MAYS 14

Varsity Publications Ltd
11-12 Trumpington Street
Cambridge CB1 1QA

First published 2006 by Varsity Publications Ltd in association
with Oxford Student Publications Ltd

ISBN number 0902240364

Typeset in Garamond
Produced by LPPS Ltd in Malta

Original Concept by Peter Ho Davies, Adrian Woolfson, Ron
Dimant

A CIP catalogue record of this book is available from the British
Library.

Further copies of this book and other titles in the series can be
bought through all good bookshops or direct from *Varsity
Publications Ltd.*, at the address above.

www.varsity.co.uk/mays

Poetry Guest Editor Don Paterson

Prose Guest Editor Jeanette Winterson

Editors   Torsten Henricson-Bell
                     Juliet Lapidos
                     Imogen Walford

Oxford Editors   Luke Alexander
                     Rowena Mason
                     Tom Pursey

Sub-editors   *Poetry*   *Prose*
                     Ruth Abbott   Henry Day
                     John Cooper   Laura Dixon
                     Catherine Fischl Laura Kaye
                     Sarah Pett   Iain Mobbs
                     James Wade   Tom Williams

Business Manager Chris Adams
Web Design   Aaron Coble
Cover Design   Tom Kingsley

With many thanks to our sponsors:

Cambridge: Churchill, Clare Hall, Fitzwilliam, Jesus, King's, Lucy Cavendish, Newnham, Pembroke, Queens', Sidney Sussex, and Trinity
Oxford: All Soul's, Corpus Christi, Exeter, Jesus, Keble, Trinity, Wolfson and all others who have supported the anthology since it went to print.

Thanks also to the Gates Cambridge Trust & Natwest (Market Street, Cambridge branch).

Thanks to: Dr Michael Franklin and the Board of Directors & Editorial Teamsat Varsity & Cherwell, Pat Dalby, Joti Madlani, Karolina Sutton and Kate Jones at ICM Books and everyone who submitted work.

Contents

Poetry

Prose

POETRY

Introduction
By Don Paterson

I'm delighted to have the opportunity to introduce this latest edition of *The Mays*, simply one of the most impressive collections of student verse it's ever been my pleasure to read. It is also an unapologetically serious book: none of these poets make the standard error of confusing writing about their feelings with writing through their feelings; the former approach always results in a sentimentality or - to use our splendid new word - an 'oversharing', and if that kind of poem leaves the house at all, it does so in an SAE. The latter, proceeding as it does from a generous, not a self-centred or proprietorial instinct, understands the first prerequisite of real art. These are generous poems, poems that were written to be read.

I was also forcibly struck by the way in which nearly all the poets here seem to be making an effort to reclaim a poetic diction, albeit using very different strategies. One simple diagnosis we can make from the fact of our steadily dwindling general readership is that most poetry just doesn't sound much like poetry anymore; readers rather preferred it when it did. Poetry is more urgent than any other kind of human speech, and it signals its urgency through its distinct diction, its originality - what Shklovskii famously called ostranenie, its 'making strange'. All the poems in this collection sound to me like poetry, but - significantly - don't sound in the least 'poetic'. As Cocteau remarked, the poet has no more need to make his poems poetic than a nursery gardener scent his roses; the poetry in these poems comes not from their affected pose but from their original stance. They all stand in an interesting relationship to the familiar world, and in doing so remake that world for us - as something at first unrecognisable, and then suddenly transformed.

Space doesn't allow me to introduce all the poets to you, alas - though I can find things to admire in all of them, and have no doubt that several of their names will become familiar to many readers over the next few years. However, I'd draw your attention to the terse and tense power of Heather McRobie's 'Red and White Flags'; Anna Wilson's neat and witty classicization of Richard Wilbur's 'The Mind Reader'; Timothy Thornton, who has written twelve poems at once, in the fashionable postmodern style - but with terrific humour, wit and speed; Tom Wells' ringing musicality; Caleb Klaces' strange minutiae, and Robert Crowe's splendid lark, 'Cornell'. All the others commend themselves to the eye and ear and mind in impressively different ways.

I've long held that publication, not merely the completion of the poem, is the poem's real goal. Without publication, the poet's relationship to the poem is improperly configured, and poems that never leave the house they were born in can eventually consume the poet with their frustration. Good poems want to be given away, to lodge themselves in the minds of other readers. All the poems in *The Mays* should feel rather pleased to find themselves in such a splendid publication, and in such excellent company.

Don Paterson was born in Dundee, Scotland, in 1963. His poetry collections include Nil Nil, God's Gift to Women, The Eyes *and* The White Lie - New and Selected Poems, *and* Landing Light. *His most recent publication is a book of aphorisms,* The Book of Shadows. *Don Paterson has been the recipient of several literary awards including the Whitbread Poetry Award, the T.S. Eliot Prize, the Geoffrey Faber Memorial Award, a Forward Prize and three Scottish Arts Council Book Awards.*

Robert Crowe

Cornell

Iago said to the elephant "I am what I am"
And Gaspacho (thus was christened our pachyderm)
replied "rubbish you're a Lear", whereupon
Pinocchio, whom we haven't yet mentioned,
Chipped in "You can talk," – a remarkable fact in itself –
"Look at that trunk". "My luggage is my business,
stringfellow". Getting haughty, that emphatic proboscis.
"I happen to be planning a long journey".
"You better not be. That is flagrant plagiarism" –
here Odysseus takes his bow – and shoots all present company
dead in a matter of minutes: a nasty habit,
but academic theft is not looked on kindly
in the University at Ithaca.

Muireann Maguire

St. Basil's Cathedral

On the completion of St. Basil's Cathedral
The tsar, jealous, blinded his architects.
No foreign prince should venture to entice
His two savants, even the mildest Tudor.
He plucked their eyeballs with the same tools
They used to flute the narrow leaping domes,
Radiant in pastels like a bruise,
The high cupolas echoing to God.
Nonetheless the pair set sail for England
Tongued salt air in puzzlement, like Hamlet,
Debarked and were granted audience
In a deep room, muttering with councillors.
As blind men will, they mimed arches
In dead space, parabolae on air.

Caleb Klaces

Goldberg and Piskey in Cornwall

Piskey has played it so much it sounds like sleep to me.

Bring a warm hat and a sewing kit,
Piskey will bring the luck, Piskey will bring his cumbersome shoes
bent up over the pedals for soft and for long.
And his big hands, tendons, worn big by precedent

you will need gloves for those hands, Piskey
embarking here you could need your camera, bring it; perhaps a kestrel
                                                will be keeping itself still

(so the world is the biggest sentence, hung off the tiniest, prettiest comma)
we will need some money,
bring your name so I can call you, unscrupulous Piskey.

For the trudge to the horseshoes and gilt frying pans and engravings
at Cawsand and Kingsand, we will want a torch,
there is only so much light tonight
for these two towns bleed into each other
like the drops of rain that are falling all over and about us,
like the Venn. Pack the big tent, we will be staying, weekending,

don't forget we will be encountering
the cat's paws at the right-angled argument of the sea and the sea will
push along the beach so fast it seems impossibly fast. At least
bring your name with you.

I am bringing the pills, speckled blue ones,
the crushed blue of the surf
they have galleons on them, a mobile army of semiquavers
it is difficult to see through the dusk
fifteen glowsticks, a packet of twenty,
two packs of Wrigley's sugarfree, whistle, keys.

Remember your name, and to keep your eyes from overleaping themselves.

When we start gnawing, I will remember your name,
metallic and bold, I will love you and ponder my hands,
your gloved hands I can't catch them
so fast it seems impossibly fast.

Over the hill I see the sea pink now,
I learnt the name of it for the walk, sea pink
doesn't leave its stalk when it is old,
unlike other flowers, it keeps its shrivel close.

Suddenly the wind my voice away from me coolly, granny sea pink
blankets her knees, Piskey scrambles,
negotiating the mosses, and it comes back to me
when we've reached the beach, brackish and dirty, with families in it and
deck chairs.

It is a girl's voice that says:

> 'I am like one of those sticks on a beach that are elephant-skinned
> from the scraggly fences bent all ways
> and skittish over dunes holding coarse grass,
> I am an old stick of hairnet' (text book)

and there are dinner ladies on the beach,
one of them holding the dribbling boy by the back of his collar.

'I am going to sleep', he is saying
and scooping a yellow drizzle-pillow
collar-hung and scuffed purchase, kicking up,
'I'll eat it'. Sand

looks like school custard,
the boy and girl have pasta with their sand;

the bottom of the car is a scrumpled thought, mind-map, brain-storm

boot up, wind up, class seven weary,
the girl gives up eating hers

looks at her boy and somewhere past his shoulder at the dribbling boy.

The bits of dribble come only to stops,
stops stops, most especially at the elephant feet of those old sticks
that find themselves leaning all at funny angles, plot-skittish, marking
something, themselves;

flaunts of horses trotting along, poppy seeds trotting, dotting spotty fields,
the sight of the dribbler and Piskey still hollering;

the sallows of the shallow fields and jaundiced gorses,
with sand in our trousers;
Piskey dotting, fireworksup hush, popping.

Next day we look around the Cornish museum,
thatched, thick bungalow with boxes of fluorescent rubbers
on a comedown, lifeboat moored outside,
feeling city clever, intruders etc.

Pooja Agrawal

Daisy Black

Interior
On a painting by Degas.

Quietly, the glow of a rose smothered lamp
Proclaims their scene. The iron prison barred bed
Stark against the floral-saccharine damp
Of walls that enclose, on atmosphere fed.

Willing voyeurs, we covet their silence.
Seeing her slip tear; the slender white girl
Caught forever muscle-knotted and tense.
Trapped between shadows, revealing the pearl

Of her shoulder and cheek. Back towards him.
Clothed in a thick smog of dark; intense strands
Cast shadows, his black bores into her skin.
Against a door locked forever he stands.

The mirror won't reflect the light of haze
That severs them; their postures acquired
A title that merely thickens the maze
Of questions. Are you weeping or tired?

They'd dance when alone, if we could know what
He demands, but knowledge would cling sordid
Like sinking hands in a soft silken knot
And coming out blood. Don't tear the boarded

Room from under their feet. Leave the sheets smooth;
Uncrumpled. Only stand there for hours
Asking and forcing what you cannot prove,
Pulling apart their desolate flowers.

Tom Wells

The River Humber's Elegy

At night, the lights of industry transformed
By dusk take on the quality of loss, of wraiths
Across an estuary of vapours, shimmering.

Freighters, dull. Ferries decked in festival
Pass, and in their passing and their poise remain
Aloof, maintain a proper distance. The noise

Of the foghorn, redundant in a dusk so crystalline,
And only this is heard. A low whale moan, an uttered truth
Alone, and shudder deep, and without words.

Denise Dooley

The Churn Game

overturned our bicycles, tricycles, big wheels,
learned a tripod of seat and handlebars, sat square
before it, spun the pedals with our hands. Kindling arms
tore circles, push till the spin wins, the whir and

coal seam smell of black tires. Shouting out sing song
"Ice cream, fresh ice cream, come n getcher ice cream."
faster, churn faster! shrieking girls. What on earth. I wonder
sister, where did we get this? We had square sidewalks on hot

square blocks ringing armoured cities - we never once saw the stuff
prepared. It came to us, when it came to us, in a picture on a
musical truck, a hard bright cube, sharp edged and wrapped up,
stuck through with a balsa wood handle. Our block knew no

rock salt or hand cranks. More like landscaping mulch, our crouching in
hot spaces behind couches, crumbling yellow chalks, the realest of all
were the long glass studded strips of tar sealing the street, soft as
fir sap in the heat. All else we invented, choke churning words

clacking out between our missing teeth, our little gums, like cable car
tracks pull loads up hills. One word holding the next. Not
talking but the act of touching oneself to feel oneself, the point of
sucking thumbs. Gear cogging sounds between us making globes,

child prattle skyward from sunburned bellies. Always put to bed in
mild early evening, the drawn paper shade sucking and
fretting against the window sill, the sirens and cicadas just
getting going, our bath damp bodies stacked in our

small beds, talking at each other and at the ceiling
all that wet mouthed dreamaloud. Pink sheets gathering
stains of spittle spots which diagram tomorrow's
games, the light going bluer and bluer and then

gone, engines start next door, algae piles quietly in the lakes, how
long does it take a child to fall asleep in summer? Can't say. Too hard to
land in this space, too interchangable. 'I' slips from my large
hand, lost who it was, which voice small crying into that shared dark.

Paul Abbott

A Bee-swarm in Summer
(On a Supermarket)

Oh dear, dear England, idiotic
and beautiful as a child is shy:
    recall that calm, idyllic
summer in a flax-field, when I
in the faint murmur of a storm
sudden, like a tentative disease
lazy-flitting, in an angry swarm
    glimpsed a billion warm
hairy orbs of black-golden bees.

I caught an isolated bee in vain,
I closed a tight fist on it, flying
    like a quick, sharp pain:
as it struggled it flew off dying.
And now I cannot quite forget,
miserable, dismal by this sight
of a drab, unquiet supermarket:
    and still vague, I regret
haunting its dim alleys at night.

Its hexagonal, fluorescent light
like a liquid cell of honeycomb
    flickers, in a dead white,
casting off a dry shadow-gloam.
Only a shelf-stacker, industrious
at his slow task, labours uneasily
down a long aisle – monotonous
    (or repetitive, or tedious)
faced by a billion jars of honey.

A thermostat emits its low hum,
a glare, an electric hungry buzz
        as he works: cold, dumb
and wary, his skin white as wax.
Sick or sweet he has stolen here
numbed by isolation and unease,
as, idle in a deaf whorl of his ear
        he strains, strains to hear
dull lazy drones of drowsy bees.

And irritatingly, I feel lethargic
as I recall a bee ceased to exist:
        dying so weak and sick
as I closed a tight, childish fist.
Idle, in a hollow calm, fraught
by a drab supermarket I stand:
like that isolated bee I caught,
        like an acute fragment,
a bee-sting is still in my hand.

Charlotte Kingston

Untitled

The noon winter's death comes silent,
And slow the gentle murderer lays frosted gild
Like poison over the parklands, the light transmuted
Into wine bled into linen, orange swept glory
On the bellies of the clouds. Let All The World
In Every Corner Sing within itself because
Here, upon this urban hill,
Is my forever, and my always, and my end.

Timothy Thornton

Gyratory System

Purging past teeth, driven flick your light off
kiln-cracked gelling agent. Are you on MSN
mate there is to be a charge on congestion,
tomorrow belongs to circadian stimulation
of the pyrrhic nerve.

Lord Jesus hisself walked on clingy agar within
these very four residues? A sinister whimsy
hinged and bracketed, direct contravention
of local byelaws. Ship of fools! swich vertu
as a shat-on cenotaph:

No space for new messages, try breaking spine
for roadwork effect alone, who *sets* their status
to go away now please. It isn't really too much
to ask, a chordstruck plectrum fractal grasp—
so wharf me, bitch,

them brittle bones done vorsprung skyward, shot
(casually) durch ventriloquist carpal tunnel:
you have *got* to co-operate, please understand
that (clothespegging her kyrie eleison clitoris
in a pub toilet).

Calamine treatment of urban space, floating poles
kept chevrons apart. That same anaphylactic terror
tongueing empty pistachio shells, alimentary.
(And Moloch heaved to hurl his brimming sickbag
to the wretched overboard.)

Owen Holland

Anna Wilson

The Seer's Tale

Polyeidos is my name. A seer by trade,
but times are hard, and I'm not proud.
I'll sing for my supper.
What'll it be? How Rhea fed her man
a swaddled rock and saved her son? No?
A drinking song, to while away the storm?
A story, then. Look no further,
friend. I've got a few.

A young fourteen, the prince was,
hair everywhere, grey eyes, dreamy;
you know the sort.
Legs too long, and arms
not yet hardened to the sword.
Friendless, quick to shy
from slantwise looks, name-calling.
No surprise, with a family
like his. In palace towns,
whispers gather in corners like cobwebs.
He'd slip his tutors, patter
barefoot over cold stone floors
past painted walls; the musty palace
would exhale him like a sigh
through its open door.
A sweet boy; sweet name, Glaukos,
the darling of the market place
who'd barter smiles and breathy thanks
for a piece of coloured glass, an apple.
When they said he'd disappeared, I didn't blink.
"Some hiding place," I said. "Check the stables."
Really gone this time, apparently.
There was talk of some reward, a call
for interpreters of portents,

mention of a cow that changed its skin.
You'd think this king had had enough of cows.

The gods speak to us in trails of blood,
the screeching track of birds across the sky,
in goats' intestines. I translate.
Money was tight; I went along.
The beast was tethered in the court, the trophy
of some grubby farm boy, goggle-eyed.
"Mister, it were white before," he said.
Well-rehearsed, no doubt. I've seen more garden-shed,
ha'penny miracles than you could shake a sceptre at.
The tattered remnants of a searching party
drew around; a few reached out to stroke it.
"Pale at dawn, then bay, now black as soot."
The object of the reverential whispers, chubby,
blank-faced, as only a heifer
who's told it is a prodigy can be.
"Sounds like a bloody mulberry," I said.
The captain grabbed me, scruff of the neck.
"Since you're so clever," he growled,
"You can be the one who gets to look."

Introduced, I shook hands with the king.
"I've heard a lot about you."
Bollocks. I didn't have a clue.
I went to check the stables, just in case.
No errant prince; there was an owl
furious and screeching fit to murder,
scaring the horses. Mad. It broke for daylight,
dragged a roaring tail of bees behind;
made it to the trees, then twisted,
fell and hit the ground, stone dead.
Its corpse crawled with stub-winged
soldiers, like the stabbing-boys
who scour the battlefield for wounded.
They left it there, a sorry
package for the scavengers;
wings grey, like his eyes, and
soft as the down on a boy's lip.
"Oh, bloody hell," I said.

Any truant from round there
has used that path;

now I ran as quick as if a thrashing were behind me.
The bee-man keeps no dog or geese;
the gauntlet of the latch and heavy lid
is supposed to be enough. It never is.
The top was open, the vat
as tall as I remembered. I clambered up,
brushed away the humming caretakers,
and there he was. A fly in amber,
face upturned below the surface,
drowned in honey. I called for help.
It took us half an hour to pull him out.
The sickly gold slurped greedily around his waist,
the bees stung through our cloaks.
We carried him between us to the palace,
sticky hands and aching shoulders, terrified.
"I've found your son," I said.

I'm no magician; I can pick a lucky day for marriage,
slit a belly. This boy was on his way
to Hades, sticky footprints on a dusty path.
Minos stared, Pasiphae
screamed, and her half-bull bastard son
roared underground. Try telling
any father that he's lost his only son.
"Bring him back," he said, "or keep him company."

A king's son has his tomb dug out
before he's born. A beehive hole,
brick-lined, with scattered gold,
a favoured pet or two, throats cut,
and me. I'm not ashamed to say,
I screamed and begged. For my pains,
I got a spear-butt in the face.
"Magic can't be rushed," they said.
"You've time. Two days from now, we'll seal you in."
They left a lamp, and water. Generous.
I swore, cajoled,
and as the guards bricked off the daylight
called on every god I knew:
Father Zeus; Poseidon, wall-breaker;
Athene, quick to anger,
and Apollo of the bow
who heals all wounds.
When my voice gave out, I cried.

They'd only sponged him down; bad luck
to dress a corpse for death before you're sure.
He could have been asleep, but for his eyes,
wide open, glazed. I lay beside him,
soaked his shirt with tears, slapped his face.
Weak, half-crazed with death, I licked
the honeyed creases of his neck, behind his ears,
knees, arse-crack, scoured his skin
for sweetness, life. I could have drunk his blood.
Mad, reeling, I swore I'd make
his father curse the day he'd left me
with the precious body of his son – I'd maim
his corpse, defile him so that even dogs
would slink away, disgusted. I'd wait
for Minos by the Styx, and when
his time came, with bloody grin
I'd tell him how I used his boy.
I climbed atop the prince;
The lamp-fire flickered, and I could have sworn
I saw a smile in the crooked shadows
of his mouth. I kissed his candied lips
and felt a breath choke and stir between them,
a heartbeat sputter into life beneath my palm.

I heard the footsteps of no bright-skinned god, but
Lord Apollo breathes my incense once a week;
I'm no ingrate, nor a fool.
I told the guards a story of a magic leaf,
two snakes, and how one
roused the other. They didn't get it.
The king clapped me on the shoulder, took
me aside. "No hard feelings?"
None, I said. He hired me.
"Teach him all you know," he said.
I did. Bullish Minos' heir, at seventeen,
could rival any kohl-eyed temple whore for tricks
of the trade, fey, adept
at horoscopes, quack potions, charms.
When he outgrew his tutor
I gave notice. He came to see me off.
I took one last kiss from him and watched him
bat his eyelids at the sailors. I left the king
a pretty witch's boy, pure sweetness of his youth

sucked dry, good for nothing.
An oath, once made,
binds tighter than affection;
The deathless ones love vengeance, nothing else.
There's your tale, moral
thrown in for free.
Another cup? Why, thank you.
Long life to you, fate willing.
Tell your friends; I'm here
every night from six. It's been
a pleasure.

Heather Mcrobie

Red and White Flags

And if I have been unkind
to your snowing places of peace:
to your Geneva
to your Canada
with your factual flags
with your questioning lakes,
If I have made dirty jokes
at your treaties and entreaties
at your German-efficient French,
It was only because I knew
that you knew
that my refugees were bogus,
that I did not have the requisite documents
and all my white papers were burnt.
That if you let me build a home in your snow
a soft red would soon seep to the borders.

Bianca Jackson

Buffalo Soldier

My tongue-less mother
Steals consonants and vowels,
Slipping them into her purse
At dinner parties
Like polished silverware.

Later, wine and smoke swirling
Down the drain,
She fingers their edges,
Saws off branches of our family tree
With a steak knife.

Born with a spoon in my mouth,
Its crest rubbed clean,
I mimic my mother's words,
Until even she forgets
They not her own.

PROSE

Introduction
By Jeanette Winterson

When I was an undergraduate at Oxford, I wrote prose so terrible that it was only fit for the fire – and that is where I put it, in a fit of La Boheme.

A few years later, by the time I was 23, I was able to write Oranges Are Not The Only Fruit.

Sitting in New York, at the PEN World Voices festival, writing this introduction, I asked Martin Amis what his stuff was like before he published The Rachel Papers. 'Unseaworthy', was the reply.

The fact is that no matter how gifted or talented you are, you need the fourth dimension, which is time.

Time, of course, is not constant, and a year for me, might be a month for you, or it might not. I left home at sixteen and fended for myself. I had a lot to handle, before, during, and after Oxford, and that makes a difference to the way time passes, and to the way in which time helps us to find a language for what we need to say.

When I talk about my own work being only fit for the fire, I do not mean it was illiterate or badly written, I mean it was unformed. I had not found my own voice, and I had not found the line of my own experiment.

That takes time.

The Mays is a good thing. It is a place of opportunity, ambition, possibility, and challenge.

I don't think the fame 'n fortune youth culture we are living through right now helps new literature, or new writers. There is too much self-consciousness, too much emphasis on getting a deal and making a name. In all of that, the simple pleasure of sitting down and writing, becomes secondary. It becomes a means to an end, and not an end itself.

The Mays should be an open forum. It should be a place to begin, in the full knowledge that any writer is always beginning, because there is always a new struggle.

The work here is full of possibility, and the writers deserve encouragement. All writers need to develop quietly for a while, without any spotlight, without any razzamatazz. The real ones will emerge.

And I hope to God that none of the writers here rush straight out of university and onto a Creative Writing course. Remember Socrates; 'the unexamined life is not worth living', and remember the graffiti, 'the unlived life is not worth examining.'

You must have something to write about that means life and death to you. You have to write from a place of authenticity – deep feeling, a kind of wound.

Without this urgency, self-consciousness will always take over, and self-consciousness is not the same as self-knowledge.

To be a writer is to put everything that you are in the service of the work that you are doing. And to be a writer demands both intensity and truthfulness. This is not a place to play games or to be half-hearted.

Does our culture encourage any of this? No.

And *The Mays*? *The Mays* needs to remain a place where young writers can begin to become themselves.

We need to support young writers – and the best way to do that is to give them space without pressure, attention without expectation, and time to allow the quantum change to happen.

And above all, we need them to believe that they are necessary. *The Mays* is part of keeping writing necessary.

Jeanette Winterson wrote her first novel, Oranges Are Not The Only Fruit, *when she was 23. It was published a year later in 1985. She is the author of numerous other works of fiction including* The Passion, Sexing The Cherry, The Powerbook, *and most recently,* Weight. *Jeanette Winterson has won various awards including the Whitbread Prize, UK, and the Prix d'argent, Cannes Film Festival.*

Ross Perlin

The Minarets of Manhattan

Two weeks after it started, my girlfriend Ann and I decided to go to the top of the Empire State Building. We had a thermos of coffee and earmuffs to keep away the cold. There was no line to enter that impossible elevator which carries you up for so long without stopping. We were alone inside it, laughing and kissing, our prayer mats tucked under our arms.

We knew that no one else would be there; no one would even be on the streets. Since the first calls, New Yorkers had lived in bleak alarm, tourists had ceased their traffic with the city, store-owners would draw down their steel shutters and turn up their radios. The worst were calls in the early morning, 4 or 5 a.m. The TV news would warn us the night before.

We reached the 102nd floor. Ann giggled as I pushed her out of the elevator and whispered, "Hurry!" I played with the headscarf she'd put on and told her how beautiful it made her look. "Chaste and pure! As beautiful as Fatima, daughter of the Prophet." She scowled a smile at me.

The wind was blowing wildly—I almost felt my neck would snap, or Ann fly away, she looked so light and rarefied. Around the platform we checked those funny view-finder telescopes, did we really need to put quarters in to see out? The city was toylike, as from a plane. Central Park looked like a front lawn. We felt like kids. I kissed her, like in a movie. "I love you, Ann." "I love you, Ross."

Then it began, and we felt shivers go down our backs. Looking at her, I unrolled my prayer rug, a tourist trinket from Istanbul I never thought I would use. She unrolled hers: from a flea market on 6th Avenue. Only then did we realize that neither of us knew what to do, except to kneel and prostrate our bodies the way we'd seen men do in mosques, or sometimes on the street in a Muslim country. A mosque can be anywhere a Muslim is, I remembered reading.

It was beautiful facing east towards the reflected sunset, across to Queens where the sky was open and golden, knowing that Mecca lay beyond. When the full surge of noise hit us, it seemed to come from the lightning rod itself. *Allahu Akbar! Allaaaaaaahu Akbar!*

When the Muslim call to prayer, as if from absolutely nowhere, began to ring out one day over the famous skyline of Manhattan in the middle of January in the year 20__, the immediate reaction was hysteria. Most people only dimly knew what it was they were hearing; those who did, or who grasped it soon enough, suspected the work of terrorists. It was so loud that all street life ceased.

I was lying in bed nursing a hangover with coffee when I first heard it. "What's that?" Ann asked from the other room. The sound had no one single source but, so it seemed, infinitely many. Once raised in one corner of the island, the call was taken up everywhere, in blinding succession.

I looked into the street below, where everyone had stopped. The call was rising up across the city, or descending from impossible heights, both from the skyscrapers and wafting over them, one call starting up after the other to give the impression of a vast chamber of echoes, the recorded full-throated cries of a million muezzins, deafening and incomprehensible, sending pigeons flying madly in every direction while people stood as if secretly murdered by the holy call to worship Allah.

Louder than the muezzins of Cairo, Istanbul, and Teheran combined, the faceless muezzins of New York sang with a dark baritone fury that was both shocking and beautiful.

"The TV'll know," I said finally. By the time I found the news channel, the Mayor had declared a state of emergency. The President was evaluating the situation; the air force was about to deploy jets. In some parts of the city, people were panicking, fleeing from their offices down endless stairs.

"The likely prelude to an attack by Islamic militants-" "Definitely the work of Al Qaeda, or one of its collaborators-" "Terrorists strike New York again-" These were the words from the television, and naturally I believed them. Ann sat openmouthed and watched them discuss the fate of our city. Loved ones called and we reassured them: "Yes, we're ok. We love you too."

Then the onslaught seemed ready to begin. Just as the prayers had subsided without incident, huge sweeping noises cut across the sky.

But the F15's were ours. Now the President was talking on every channel, lots and lots of concocted noise. Thousands of people were springing to action across the world, collecting intelligence, studying the soundpatterns of the calls to prayer, listening in on the secret code of Qur'anic terror and violence. All night and all the next day the F15's cruised overhead burning their fuel into the clouds. The prayer kept returning, five times each day, but there was nothing else to find. Only the sound of the word of Allah. Right on schedule every time, according to the imams they interviewed on TV.

Although the state of emergency continued all week, and the counter-terror plans went into effect, I finally ventured out to see if I could buy some groceries. "After all, nothing violent has happened!" I said to Ann. "But isn't something bound to?" she replied. "Something like this doesn't just happen."

We had both stayed glued to the TV. Speculation #1 from the pundits: terrorists had clambered their way to the tops of our sky-scrapers and set up a broadcast system of tremendous power. Acoustics experts denied this, saying that the volume of the call was at an unbelievable level, impervious to scientific explanations. And apparently soldiers had done a thorough check of the major buildings and discovered nothing unusual. Nothing unusual, it was repeated again and again between advertisements, but we're investigating.

Out on the street, only the Muslim-owned stores were open. These weren't many, but the atmosphere of joy was palpable. Prayer rugs had been left out on the corner of 47th and 2nd, outside our favorite Lebanese restaurant—the men who used them for prayer were now drinking tea with sugar and laughing. The owner saw me and went slightly pale.

"*Salaam Aleikum*," I greeted him. He smiled nervously, "*Wa'alekum Salaam*."

"What's going on?" I asked as unassumingly as I could.

"To us... well, we do not know," he glanced behind at his friends.

"Well, what do you think of all the terrorist groups that have tried to claim responsibility?"

"Ridiculous," he said with disdain. He stared at me with a fixed expression- "Some of us believe that maybe it is God himself, God calling on New York to worship Him."

People started going out again in the intervals between the calls to prayer. The government, mired in "a serious investigation", was clearly out of the picture, and life would have to go on somehow. Those who could not stand it left the city. Even in Brooklyn Heights the sound was much quieter, and by the time you reached Midwood you couldn't hear it at all. Others thought it would pass in a few weeks at most.

Only the Christians knew what to do. The day after the prayers started, Christian leaders across the country were convening their flocks and praying to their God to save New York. Pat Robertson went on a prayer fast, so did Billy Graham—calling on God to take the voice of the infidel god from our ears.

Soon they were arriving in the city, in trucks and vans, carpool-ing from the edges of the country with huge banners on their cars, a signature honk, pleated pants. The Mormons chartered planes from

Salt Lake City. They were all ready to do battle.

Their weaponry was various. Counter to my instincts, I admired them. Some had hefted the largest, most state-of-the-art Japanese speakers available and extension cords that could stretch for blocks. The city and its shopkeepers opened their electrical outlets to these crusaders. Some simply prayed, discerning world's end in the imams' throats. Children's choirs sang, men preached and called upon the Lord. All perfectly timed to meet the muezzins' calls as they drifted and swam around the Chrysler Building's cathedral spire, the right-tri-angle-top of the Citicorp Center, the tall blocks stretching up in the International Style.

Ann and I would go into the streets to watch the Christians. I told her of the Berbers described by Ibn Khaldoun who dressed in full battle gear to make war with winds from the Sahara. We laughed and cried at it all, quit our jobs, stole things because no one seemed to care. This city seemed made for us, at the mercy of a miracle, in the grip of sound warfare. We didn't care what we did, so long as we were somewhere good to hear the call to prayer. To keep from getting bored we did different things—smoked weed, got drunk, sang along with it, recorded it from the bridges, danced to it.

The Christians were losing. Even as reinforcements kept arriv-ing from England, from Arizona, from New Guinea, from Africa. When people grew frustrated to hear the name of Jesus drowned out by the name of Allah, they played *muzak* to the skies. Nobody else could mount much of a group effort; all the city did was pass out Swedish-made earplugs at every street corner. Mad scientists counte-nanced a vast "sound blanket" to drape New York in silence.

We had no use for any of it. Each day it grew more and more beautiful, the calls lasted longer. I was leaving the Mid-Manhattan Library one day with Ann—our arms were full of books on Islamic law, Burton's pilgrimage account, Qu'ranic exegesis—and, in the full-blast-trumpet moment of the divine noise, everything fell from our arms and we knelt in the middle of the 5th Avenue pavement. The next day we went to the Empire State Building.

The city was just beginning to empty out when the first pilgrims arrived. As word spread of the grace Allah had shown New York, of the new terrifying beauty, people throughout *Dar Al-Islam* saved their earnings, made plans, boarded planes to come to the heart of the mir-acle. Dressed like *hajjis* came the Malaysians, the Saudis, the Jordanians, unrolling their prayer rugs across Central Park, Union Square, along the East River Promenade. The government could not stop them from coming. The mosques couldn't hold them all. Ann preferred to pray in the streets, but I joined a mosque on 96th Street, a beautiful light stone and marble structure ringed by parked taxi cabs. I nodded and smiled in my few words of Urdu, but my prayers were perfect.

There must have been others like us—were there? No one could have been transfixed the way we were. Our remaining friends were leaving the city. Drunk at goodbye dinner parties (for I still drank then), I would insist that everyone stay and celebrate, that this was the most beautiful thing possible, what we had always longed for. It was an ugly way to separate. Ann dragged me from those parties. Sometimes our friends would be dancing and drinking and talking when the call would come through the windows (mechanically they would put in their earplugs and shut the windows) and everyone would stay silent until it stopped. Only Ann and I would stay as we were, looking at each other in a kind of rapture. We closed our eyes.

Two months had passed. The Christians were leaving. The government had discovered nothing, but they were bombing somewhere. Businesses were leaving; who could do business in such a place? Every day our city became more and more a citadel of Islam. Some fine morning the muezzin's call became normal.

One afternoon I sat in the back office of the 96th Street mosque after prayers and spoke with the imam about Islam. He was transfixed by the same fear and joy that gripped all Muslims in New York at that moment: would riots begin? would the city truly be handed over to Islam? have we reached the end of days?

He spoke quietly about the coming troubles in the city, the seething range of those displaced, the rage of America. "But the ring of God's voice will even float over the smoldering ruins," I recall him saying. "They cannot destroy what is from God."

And it was on that strange grey afternoon that we spoke of my making the *hajj* to Mecca and Medina. Ann could not, would not. We had been fighting about it. She prayed unevenly, kept drinking and smoking, and she was beginning to panic too. Yet I had never felt so much at peace before.

The mosque would sponsor my visa, yes. We would go as a group. Yes, in a month's time. *Insha'allah* all will be well until then.

On my last day in New York, the city seemed finally to have become holy. Skyscrapers transformed into minarets. Remaining business executives frightened and trapped in the top floors, like unwilling muezzins. Lost princesses of the former regime. I could imagine the alleys and caverns of lower Manhattan a vast *souk*. New York, just maybe, had been made for this. A fitting capital for the caliphate, for the end of days.

Such a tiny miracle, I thought, God barely lifting his finger to change the shape of human history. Could anyone now doubt how universal is the Muslim call to prayer? How much effort we would all have been spared if only the call had come earlier. In my own heart, I believed that the call would spread. This was only its beachhead.

I got on the subway to the airport. The A was empty, so was the AirTrain. As we rattled over Williamsburg, I heard what I thought were the distant echoes. I could only close my eyes and begin to dream of Mecca.

We all wait for something supernatural to take place. As a boy, I used to wonder what it would be—a homeless man walking on top of the Hudson River, a tenement that a blazing fire leaves untouched, the dead of Greenwood Cemetery coming back to life? It always seemed that the moment was just about to come, and that afterwards everything would have to be different.

Now, as I look back over three months, I realize that that the moment I waited for, the event my life was leading up to, has come and gone. Knowing what I must do only dulls the sadness of knowing this.

I'm sitting now, waiting in Terminal 6 at John F. Kennedy International Airport for Gulf Air flight 166 to Medina, connecting through Dubai. My friends from the mosque will be here soon. Will they be impressed to see the bilingual Qu'ran in my lap? My white skullcap? My beard is just starting.

In and out of a thin layer of dreaming, I envision the minarets of Manhattan. I dream of Mecca. I cannot distinguish the two. What was my life, before? In the capital of my life, in the city that is my home, in the center of the world, we have received a new beginning. Of course the world had turned its back. As bombs dropped, I could be saved. The muezzins would soon sing from towers in every city, in every world.

With my eyes half-closed and my soul at peace, I find it impossible to make sense of the sudden bustle around me. Why is everyone cheering, hugging each other, crying? And I see a few dark men looking sad. What is that hysterical woman shouting on her cell phone, *They've stopped! Thank god they've stopped.*

Alex Steer

The Invisible Kingdom

'Ours are but moments,' the Reverend Ball was saying; and at the back
of the classroom, with its chessboard grid of ancient pitted desks and
those high windows that lit up the chalk-dust however many miles
above his head, Michael struggled against the weight of his eyelids.
'Always remember that, boys. We are but the briefest creatures in the
long story of God's work, His salvation for mankind, and we disap-
pear from this life and return into His care soon enough after. But
while we are here, here on this earth, it is beholden—'

It was Tuesday, and Tuesday meant Religious Instruction, and
what Michael did not hear, he knew already, for four years at school
and Sunday church had taught him that this was old Ball's favourite
theme. Somewhere between hearing and recollection a bellowed '*sic
transit gloria mundi*' floated like a woeful ghost, and in his mind drifted
out the window and down the street, past the church and Mrs
Brocket's shop, and all across the Sussex countryside, and down the
lanes to the sea, where it turned into a ship full of grim-faced men
who abandoned England and all her absent glories, and set sail for the
East.

'We may look at the world,' the Reverend was saying as
Michael's eyes flicked open again and he drew back from the edge of
dreaming to notice that the tired grey man in his worn black shirt had
produced the globe. It was an ancient piece in wood and leather, older
even than its owner, 'with all the oceans properly depicted' (as it was
written in the middle of the Pacific), and the countries and their cap-
itals—some of them places that no longer existed, nor had done since
the Great War—neatly stencilled onto its brown and gold and
turquoise surface. Michael adored it, for its look and its smell and its
fragile touch, but most of all for those names, those coastlines and
deserts and mountain ranges, the endlessness of places he had never
seen, except on that old globe's creaking sphere.

'Yes, we may look at the world, and think it wide and strange
and hostile and fearful. But I tell you in the eyes of heaven this world
is but a small, small place, and every part of it is known; and to the

Lord and His angels, for whom a thousand years are as a day, what a tiny place the world must be compared to the great vaults of heaven. How small, then, we must seem.'

Reverend Ball's rough fingers, with their film of dust and India ink, walked over the mountains and the seas like the giants in the land of Canaan, and Michael imagined their arrogant progress flattening forests, and crushing sleeping towns. It wasn't right, he thought, to speak of the world that way.

A boy raised his hand. 'Yes, Evans?'

'God's angels, sir. Where do they live?' There was a brief shimmer of suppressed mirth from the other boys, but Michael fixed his eyes upon that globe. The Reverend was wearing his patient face, but his eyes let them all know he would not be wearing it long.

'The angels—now listen close to this—live in a kingdom that you will not find anywhere in this world. Now it tells us in our Old Testament that once the angels walked about on this earth, but the sins of Man put paid to that. So you may set off today and walk'— and as if to demonstrate he gave the globe a spin— 'all the way from here to Australia and back again, but you will not find the kingdom of the angels. Now, boys, does anybody know the name of that kingdom?'

Michael stared at that globe, at its ancient boundaries and forgotten names, and at that moment, he realised, he knew.

'Parfitt, yes?'

'Is it the Austro-Hungarian Empire, sir?'

—cords it all? How clever. Oh, I think it's started. Should I?

My name is Ellen Brocket, I am sixty-nine years old and a retired grocer of this parish. This here's the song of the Princess and the Fairy, only it's not a song so much as it's a story, as was told to me by my grandmother.

Oh, yes, sorry, love. As recorded on the twelfth day of August, nineteen thirty-nine for Georg—

How was it again? Straussmann? Straussmann. Of the department of phil-ol-o-gy, is that right? Cologne University.

Right, so you should know as how this is an old old story from when the world was young and there were no churches in England nor any such. And there was this man as had this daughter, and that daughter of his was right beautiful but always off straying, which is never a good thing for any young woman to do if you ask me.

After classes were evening prayers and the daily lesson, and it was dark before Michael escaped from the assembly hall's heavy shadows into the higher, clearer blackness of an August night. Hanging overhead, turning slowly like cogs in a clock, were more constellations than he could name (and he knew enough, for his father had taught him them once, their English and Latin forms, and they had made up new names for most of them too, camped out in the meadow behind the Falcon and Flag); and down the lane stretched all the lights of the village, lights he had always known and trusted to guide him home, and which like the constellations would not go out.

He ran, not because it was dark but because it was cold, and he had no coat. They all ran, a great scuffed, dirtied trail of shapes in ill-cut flannel streaming down towards the village square like grey paint spilled in water. Evans was beside him, talking in breathless bursts.

'Parfitt—how's the arch—arch-duke and—duchess?'

'Shut up, or I'll trip you.'

'Wouldn't—dare. Even if you are—pally with the arist—ocra-cy.'

Michael tripped him, to prove the point, and to watch him stumble bulkily before regaining his stride. 'Scab,' Evans said, and elbowed him half into a hedge. 'What was chapel? I—wasn't listening.'

'He did the angel coming to Mary again. I like it.'

'You *like it?*' echoed Evans. '*Why?*'

They were nearing the square now, and Michael stopped sharp. Evans decelerated with a series of inelegant movements and the sound of rubber soles scudding against the ground.

'I'll show you,' Michael said, turned, and shot off down a path that crossed that of the now vanishing, quietening crowd.

Evans shrugged, composed himself, and followed.

Now, her father, he would say to her, You may go where you like down in the village—villages back then being much the same, I suppose, as they are now—but no matter what don't go straying to the edge of the wood. For the wood, you see, was dark and strange and beyond the bounds, and the wood was where the fairies dwell.

They moved slowly, curling themselves around the barely open door and into the silence of the darkening church. Only the central aisle was visible; beyond that, it stretched into a lampless emptiness that might have gone on forever. Parfitt went first, his eyes fixed on the distant prospect of the high altar, the pulpit and lectern. Evans glanced about, tracking as his only points of reference every shadow set flickering by the few low-burning candles that made the air taste hot and thick. He remembered stories he had heard of great explorers, gazing upon the mysteries of the tombs of long-dead Egyptian kings. But he came here every Sunday morning; and Howard Carter's mother wouldn't have had his guts for going where he wasn't allowed. And still the world beyond the aisle seemed to have melted away, and everything was strange.

'We're not meant to be here,' he whispered, and the shadows whispered back. Parfitt shushed them. He had said nothing since they'd arrived, but his eyes shone with something Evans didn't have a name for.

They had reached the pulpit, and Parfitt was climbing the steps. Each footfall was accompanied by a series of cracks and wails of ancient wood that threw themselves up into the darkness and came raining back down. He was taking something—a book—down from the small collection that gathered dust up there. Every step of his return was an agony of fractured sounds as Evans waited for him at the bottom. Someone was bound to come—Reverend Ball, the warden, a grown-up, any grown-up—and they would be shouted at and dragged off home to a wrath more terrible than any god could manage. *For there are no things in heaven or on the earth or under the earth*, thought Evans to himself, *more bloody scary than your mum when she's mad.*

'Look.' Parfitt was sat on the edge of the lowest step, within the candle's faltering circumference, and with the book open before him. 'John, *look*. There, that's why. There.'

It was the Children's Illustrated Bible, the one they used in Sunday School. On the page was a coloured etching, a picture of a man. He was tall and thin, dressed in a white robe, out from which the artist had drawn a splay of thin, almost perfectly straight lines as if to show a bright light. His hair was yellow and his eyes were blue, and his arms were stretched out to a young woman who knelt before him. Evans read the words that were printed below them.

'Hail, thou that art highly favoured. The Lord is with thee, Luke.'

'She's not Luke. That's Mary. And that's the angel.'

'Oh.'

'He's beautiful. Isn't he beautiful?'

Evans looked at the angel. He was a man, and men weren't beautiful; men were strong and brave and they did things, they didn't stand there pointing. 'I suppose so. He looks tall.'

'He's the most beautiful thing I've ever seen in any book or anywhere. I'd love to see an angel.'

Evans shook his head and his eyes widened. 'No you wouldn't. If you saw an angel it'd mean he'd come for you. And what if he had bad news? Or what if he *was* bad news and was going to take you away to hell and it was the angel of death or the last trump in the Revelation and you weren't one of the ones God wanted from His book and they wouldn't let you in and you had to go into the lake of fire and that all because you'd broke into His church and stolen one of His books? What'll we do then?'

And to the relief of Evans' immortal soul, Parfitt dropped the book and ran, and they both ran and they didn't speak and they didn't stop running until they were down the lane and past the lights and lamps and in through their doors and up to their dining tables where they washed their hands and sat and ate and uttered not a word, and said extra long graces at the start and the end of it, just to make sure.

See, the world back then, or so authority says, was a fairer and more noble-ish place than it is these days, and back then as they say there was such things as real love and beauty in the world not like there is now, as it goes. Not sure that I believe that all that much, but there's the tale as she's told it. Biscuit?

Sorry, where was I? Oh yes. And all that beauty and love attracted the attention of the habitants of that fairy world whose entrance lies in the woods, and who are beautifuller than us all and have no names and cannot be seen but hardly ever.

All the rest of that week Michael saw angels in his sleep, strange beautiful men coming to him in the night with dark purposes; and as he sat in class he would wonder whether each equation solved, each sentence parsed, would be his last, and whether some being from on high was even now tracking his minute progress over the surface of the globe, eventually to find him and catch him as he struggled with his declensions. Extra diligence in Religious Instruction did nothing to allay his fears, and that lack of peace convinced him that the Lord God, who was among other things (so said Reverend Ball) both 'jealous' and 'right swift to avenge', had set Himself and all His kingdom (which, he knew now, was neither Austro-Hungary nor the Ottoman Empire, nor Bechuanaland nor the fruitless-sounding Orange Free State for that matter) against him alone. At times he would stare at the globe and wonder if there were any part of it that God did not know about. Turkey, he had noticed, was not labelled, and was perhaps a good bet. Thinking like that, though, would only mean more trouble, should God find out.

Now it happened as this young girl she was ignoring her father's instructions, and went walking down by the edge of the wood. And as she was there a fairy prince rode by on a white horse, and his hair was fair and his eyes were blue, and clear as day he was one of them from that invisible kingdom. And he looked on her and she looked back there on him. And that beauty of his stole her heart clean off, because she knew she could never have him for he was of another world, and there was none fairer in this one.

An early fall of leaves in the meadow behind the inn brought some relief, and for hours after school he could lose himself in the deep crisp smell of them, the earthy taste that smell left in the mouth, and the crackling beauty of their umbers and burnt siennas as he would lift, kick, hurl and re-gather, always forgetting the damage to his clothes; or the lateness of the hour until the sun would drain out of the low clouds and beckon him home for tea; or the looming fear of some supernatural intelligence.

On the Friday evening, when he had succeeded in burying himself entirely beneath a shroud of dead foliage, the solitude of his cell was disturbed by a voice that cut through the long grass from the roadside gate. He lifted his head, disturbing a cairn of leaf-mould, and saw his father, still dressed in the suit he wore to the bank, and carrying his umbrella and copy of the *Times*, and smiling as if he were remembering, or looking at something very far away.

'Michael!' And Michael ran over and took his father's hand, and his father brushed the leaves from him. 'Best smarten you up. Come on, let's head for home. There's someone there you should meet.'

They walked, but Michael remembered little of the journey. His mind was already in their small house, looking for its new acquaintance. There had been talk of sending him to boarding school, perhaps at Lancing down on the coast, though that would not be for another four years, when he would be thirteen. As they passed down the garden path and his father turned the key in the red front door, and even more as they stepped through into the hallway, the competing suggestions in Michael's mind seemed to cancel each other out and leave it blanker than before.

Now time came when that old man decided to find a husband for his daughter, for she was of an age. And so he went to the lord, as owned all the land from halfway here to the sea, and he begged him to take his daughter, and the lord having heard tell of how beautiful she was consented, and he rode to the man's house to take her back to his estate. But the young woman she looked at him once and she looked at him twice, and she said no she would not marry him, for though rich he was not fair, and she refused, which was an odder thing back then than even now.

His mother was in the kitchen: he could hear her. Between mealtimes and bedtimes he experienced his mother chiefly as a series of sounds, the noise of fervent works in far-off rooms, and at any other times as a flicker of passing cotton or cheesecloth, the click of shoes and the murmur of occasional jewellery.

The living-room was small, adjoined the dining room and was centred on the fireplace, a squat heavy thing like a goblin that sat in the middle of the long wall and would occasionally spit heat (though never enough) towards the beige suite that huddled around it, holding back just far enough to allow for a small coffee table. On the mantelpiece were a few books, a vase with a crack down the side that was turned to the wall, an ash-tray and his father's pipe and tobacco; above it were an old photograph of lots of people in suits and frocks, with a man who looked like his father standing next to a young woman in a big white dress, and a map of the world.

Sitting in one of the beige armchairs, reading a book, was a man in a dull green suit. The man looked up, and his eyes met Michael's. He was tall, thin. He had fair hair and pale skin and the bluest eyes Michael had ever seen. He smiled. He was beautiful. Like—

'Michael, this is Georg,' said his father. *Yay-orgh*. It was a name Michael had never heard before, beautiful and impossible, strange and terrible like the names of those Canaanite giants. 'He's visiting the village, and will be staying in the spare room for a while. He's from... where was it you were from, I'm sorry?'

'Prussia, I suppose,' said the man.

'Really?' said Michael's father, sitting in the other chair.

'Well, originally, of course,' said the man.

'Well, yes.' Michael's father turned to him. 'Georg's family come from a country that doesn't exist any more, you see?' He glanced up at the wall. 'So you won't find it if you look on the map.'

Michael's soul turned to lead, and sank into his legs. The last thing he heard before he ran awkwardly from the room and tried to look as though he wasn't running, was his father saying, 'He's a *philologist*. Do you know what a philologist is?'

He spent the whole evening looking through his father's books on scripture, but nowhere among the ranks of the cherubim and seraphim did he find that name.

And so this man he went out to see the greatest knight of the shire, who had fought gainst all kinds of foes here and in far-off lands and won many a tournament with his jousting and his sword, and this man he said to the knight, Will you take my daughter's hand? And the knight having heard tell of how beautiful she was consented, and he rode to the man's house to take her back to his estate. But the young woman she looked at him once and she looked at him twice, and she said no she would not marry him, for though strong in his arm he was not fair. And her father he despaired.

Well, you would, wouldn't you?

'He's come for me, John,' Michael said. 'A real angel. Just like in the book, only maybe even taller. I'll bet he's come for you, too.'

They sat on a low wall on the edge of the village square. It was a Sunday, church and Bible class over, and although the weather was turning colder it was warm enough to sit out in shirt sleeves. From here they could see the lanes in four directions, and any comings or goings through the village would pass by them. Evans was chewing on a bag of seeds, and Michael, unusually, was not.

'I didn't see him,' said Evans, in between exploratory movements of the tongue to dislodge seeds stuck in his teeth. 'Maybe He didn't see me. God, I mean. Maybe I ran too fast, or He was only looking in the pulpit.'

'You idiot. He can see everything, even in the dark. He'll come for you.'

'Maybe you're the worse sinner. Ask Reverend Ball.'

'No. Anyway, what about when I'm gone down to the fiery pits of hell and denomination? You'll be the only one left. I bet you'll be the worst sinner in the whole village!'

'I'm not!' yelled Evans. 'I'll push you!'

'You'll never! That's a sin!' retorted Michael, but the last word was lost in their cries as Evans pushed him backwards into the grass behind the wall, and Michael grabbed him and pulled him down with him.

'Sinner!' yelled Michael.

'You're the worst! You're the one stole the—'

'Ssh!' Michael was ducked behind the wall still, peering over the top and trying to flatten down his hair with his hand to improve his camouflage. 'Look! There he is!'

It was several seconds before Evans managed to look over their parapet. And there he was, the angel, as tall and as fair as the one in the book that had drawn him here in the first place. He was walking into the square, and his pace was slowing. He was stopping. 'Where does he keep his wings?' Evans breathed.

'They don't all have wings, Evans. He's a *philologist*. I think it's like an archangel.'

'And he's living in your spare room? Maybe he's got himself thrown out of—'

'Quiet!' hissed Michael. 'He's stopped. He knows we're here.' They ducked low, waited, listening for any sound. When it came, it was the sound of laughter.

Michael peeked over the wall one more time. 'He's with someone! A girl.' Then, a few seconds later, 'It's Bess!'

Evans leapt up, stared over the wall and looked at the dark-haired, dark-eyed girl in the cotton dress and shawl with a different kind of concern. 'Why's he talking to my sister?'

'Maybe he's trying to get the truth out of her. Maybe he's going to go round your house and get you while you're sleeping.'

Evans paled. 'Maybe he's got the wrong one. Michael, what if God couldn't see properly in the dark and He got the wrong one of us?' Evans stared at the angel in a suit that was talking to his sister. How could he? She was seventeen and pretty and had long hair and wore dresses and was, well, *a girl*. It made no sense at all.

'Or maybe he hasn't come for us at all. Maybe he's not an avenging angel like we thought.'

Evans tore his gaze away and stared at Michael. 'What do you mean?'

'Well, what else do angels do?' Evans struggled to remember anything from any number of Bible classes, Sunday sermons, Religious Instructions and evening prayers, but Michael got there first. 'Evans! You know!' he said.

'I don't!'

Michael looked at him and his eyes were burning again. '*Hail, thou that art highly favoured...*'

Now it happened that there was one other man of marrying age in the village, and he was a humble man, a teacher and a fellow of book-learning. And he heard tell of this young lady and he begged her father's permission to go and see her and ask for her hand. And her father refused once, and he refused twice, for the man was neither rich nor strong in arm nor owned land nor fought great victories in wars. But the teacher asked a third time, and in the end the man he consented.

The days went quicker without the constant fear of reprisals from on high, and turned into weeks. The two of them made a compact not to tell anyone else the truth about the Angel Georg, in case he didn't want anyone else to know, since that would only risk bringing his wrath down upon them. Michael saw him less and less, both in his dreams and around the house, but the intelligence from Evans was that he was still there, and had several times been seen in the village talking to Bess. The few times Michael did see him, he was walking with her, and often neither of them were saying anything, so either the angel's message was taking time to sink in, or (more likely) he was not as forward as the Angel Gabriel in St Luke's Gospel, and was taking time to compose himself before delivering the news. In either case, Bess seemed neither fearful nor trembling, which were the two things he was sure people were meant to be upon seeing an angel. Perhaps she had not noticed he *was* an angel; but how that was possible, since he was so beautiful and she had only to look in the Illustrated Bible to notice that that was exactly how they appeared, Michael did not know.

'Well, if she is,' he said to Evans as they sat in church one morning in uncomfortable collars, 'you'll be His uncle.'

'Is what?'

'You know, *highly favoured*. If she's going to bear forth a son and call his name something-or-other though she is still'—and here he dropped his voice further— 'a virgin, and not pledged to be married to anyone neither and He will be called the Son of God and that, well you'll be His uncle. And you being such a terrible sinner. You'll have to behave. I've got an angel in my house; *you'll* have the Lord God Himself!'

Evans elbowed him discreetly in the ribs. 'What's it like? Having him there I mean?'

'His room's full of all this stuff, gramophones and that, and lots of books, and something called a 'wire recorder'. I caught a look in when I knew he was out. My father says he told *him* he's come here to take down stories from all the old folks in the village.'

'Oh,' said Evans thoughtfully. 'Maybe they don't have stories of their own in heaven, and they come down here and take down ours to tell the souls of little children.'

'Maybe,' Michael replied, and thought, how sad.

And the teacher he went to the girl, and the girl she looked at him, and saw that he was fair though poor, and she said I will marry you for though not rich or strong you are fair. And the teacher threw it off as it was a disguise and was revealed, and he was the fairy prince, and richer and stronger than any man. And he took her away and they lived all happy ever after, just as you please.

There was talk in the village and it was not happy. Most of the time adult conversation was of no interest to Michael, but what he noticed first was that the wireless was always on, and the crisp perfect voices on the other end sounded sadder and more serious than usual. They said the word 'Poland' a lot, and talking about a chamberlain called Neville. Michael wasn't sure what a chamberlain was, but the word had an unsettling tripping quality, like something fragile tumbling down the stairs. After a while, as that warm August shuffled into a cooling September, there was talk of invasions and armies on the move, and Michael thought of those fingers, striding over the globe as if they owned it.

His father looked more worried these days when he returned from the bank, and he walked as if the *Times* under his arm were getting heavier. Michael would glance at the headlines, but most of them made little sense to him.

And people were talking about the Angel Georg now too. 'I suppose he'll have to go back now all this has happened,' he heard his mother say in a distant room. Back, it transpired, was to somewhere called 'Trier', which perhaps was the capital city of the kingdom of God's angels. 'I suppose so,' his father said. 'He's said as much himself, that he cannot stay. It's such a shame; his work is barely half done.'

Michael sat in the living room, in front of the ugly fireplace, and listened. Perhaps this would mean an escape from any divine vengeance. Perhaps he was too far down the list of things the angel had to do before he left; perhaps there *were* worse sinners in the village. All the same, though, if the angel did have an important message for Bess Evans, he hoped he had managed to give it to her in the end.

Leastways I think that's how it ends. Maybe it's different things in different places.
Have you heard the wireless, Georg. It's so confusing. I'm very old for all of this. I tend to forget.
Remind me why we're doing this again?

He saw the angel once more, loading heavy cases into a taxi-cab on the road. He had never thought that angels might carry baggage where they went, but it made sense of a kind. He looked sad, thought Michael, as if there were something very important he had forgotten to do. Perhaps he had not delivered his message; perhaps, simply, he had not collected enough songs. But everyone in the village looked sad these days, as if too many of their songs had been taken away. The wireless never seemed to play music any more; maybe that was why.

After that he was gone, and nobody really spoke of him again, because everybody was concerned with the wireless and the papers, and with being afraid of other countries across the sea, and Germany most of all, for some unknown reason.

A few weeks later, people were talking about Bess too, using words and expressions Michael did not understand. Only after several days, passing out of a dismal Sunday service into a cool bright autumn morning, did he hear one of the old woman saying, 'I hear she's, well, you know, 'great with child'.'

The angel had delivered his message after all. Michael smiled for Bess, and he wondered why nobody else was smiling.

He did not see her again.

Paul Castro

Ned Beauman

The Maggot and the Whore

*Milosh Obrenovic (1780-1860), Prince of Serbia, was forced to abdicate in 1839.
His eldest son, Milan Obrenovic (1818-1839), succeeded him, but was bed-ridden
with tuberculosis and died after a reign of only twenty-six days. During that time
Serbia was administrated by a regency of three noblemen, including Jevrem,
Milosh's brother.*

I am without doubt the greatest ruler that any nation has ever had or
ever will have. I have started no wars, ordered no purges, imposed no
laws, demanded no taxes. I rule Serbia better than God rules heaven. I
certainly rule better than my maggot of a father used to.

They think I don't know I'm the Prince. They think it will upset
me too much to learn that my father has abdicated and the Troika have
taken over. Unfortunately they can't get their stories straight. Ljubica,
my mother, has told me my father's away on a diplomatic mission to
Turkey and I am representing him in his absence, but Cuniberto, my
physician, has told me he's only gone to Kragujevac to deal with a
crooked bishop and everything is going on as normal. They know it
doesn't matter what they tell me because I am to die soon. Well,
Ljubica's a fat whore and Cuniberto's a shit-head Italian and I hope
they both catch consumption off me. People in this palace seem to
think that if my eyes are closed, and they affect a stage whisper, they
can say what they like to each other in my bedroom and I won't hear.
They're wrong, but I do not intend to disabuse them of that notion. In
fact, I know perfectly well that my father was taken across the Sava into
Austria by armed guards, that he is now in exile in Walachia with my
younger brother Michael, and that he was lucky not to have his head
cut off.

Actually, I may call my mother a whore, but I have met real
whores, as many as I have found time to meet in my short and blight-
ed life, and none of them are as fat as the Princess. If you're that fat,
you can't be a whore, you can only run a brothel. She's too fat to get
on a horse, even with the help of her footman. So is my uncle Jevrem's
wife. I cannot understand this predilection for fat women among the

Brothers Obrenovic. My father is one of the richest men in Christendom and he chooses a fat wife. It's baffling. Perhaps she wasn't so fat when he met her, and perhaps he wasn't so rich. Well, he should at least have looked at her mother to see if she was fat. If I ever got married, I would choose a skinny bride with a skinny mother, but thankfully I will be dead long before I have to shackle myself like that.

But I digress. I call my mother a whore because she is one. Someone ought to inscribe 'Abandon all hope all ye who enter here' over her cunt. My father is not the only doomed soul she has somehow - I can only assume through some sort of gypsy magic - tempted into her bed. She will fuck anyone. She has certainly fucked Cuniberto, her footman, all three members of the Troika, and of course my father, so, in other words, she has fucked every character so far mentioned in this account apart from her family members, herself, and God, although the peasants have a drinking-song about how she likes to masturbate with a gold crucifix which takes care of the last two. Oh, and she also hasn't fucked the crooked bishop from Kragujevac, but only, no doubt, because he's fictitious. And then there's the horse, but the less said of that the better.

The Whore once killed one of my father's mistresses. To the Maggot's credit, he knows how to find a pretty mistress. How would my mother like it if he killed one of her favourite men, I wonder? Of course, he has, very often, but for unrelated reasons. My father has killed a great many men. He has a royal monopoly on salt and cattle but life and death are just as much within his power. He kills anyone who gets in his way, and anyone who might get in his way, and anyone who he suspects of wanting to get in his way, and anyone whose name is mentioned on a rainy day when he's bored. He sometimes tries to blame it on bandits, or a tragic accident. In Serbia, if you want power, you learn to murder. The wolves in our forests have more mercy than our great men.

Michael is back from Austria. He came in just now with my mother. As they came up the stairs I heard my mother say, 'Now, Michael, you are not to say anything.'

'What if he asks where I've been? What if he asks about Father?' said my brother. 'Tell him everything's well. We will be lucky if he even realises we are with him,' said my mother.

'Are you awake, Milan?' she said as she approached my bed. I groaned as if feverish. 'Your brother is here.'

'Michael?' I murmured weakly, squinting at him.

'Hello, Brother,' he replied.

'Where have you been?'.

'In Austria.' My mother looked at him in anger.

'Austria? Why?'

'Your brother has been hunting,' my mother interrupted. 'Now you must rest, Milan. We will see you tonight.'

As they went down the stairs, I could hear my mother berating my brother for telling me part of the truth. It's obvious my brother is desperate to tell me the rest of it: he wants me to know that when I die he will be Prince, assuming the Troika can be prevailed upon to step aside. Michael is a pitiful show-off.

In recounting my charade, I do not mean to suggest that I am not ill. Every day I cough up bucketfuls of gore, and I can hardly sleep for the pain in my chest. Sometimes it's as if a demon has crawled inside me and is raking its claws over my tender flesh. I am too weak to get up, otherwise I wouldn't allow myself to be confined to this bed. I will not survive another week. But the consumption hasn't affected my thinking or my senses.

In fact, I've done my best to exercise my mind in the last few weeks. Unfortunately, I have found few worthy objects to which to turn my unblunted mental faculties. Kodorovic, one of my father's pet bureaucrats, goes often to Vienna, where he was educated, and he brings me back books, probably in the mistaken belief that I will put in a good word for him with my father (or these days I suppose with my brother). Let me tell you my opinion on modern European letters. It is all shit. Pushkin: shit. Goethe: shit. Balzac: shit. Lermontov: shit. Hugo: shit. Hegel: irredeemable shit. Kant: dear God, truly irredeemable shit. I could do much better than any of them if I had the patience. Often I regret that I ever allowed that bald charlatan Isailovic to teach me French and German. Kodovoric tells me it is now very fashionable for English poets to get consumption like me. I think that tells you all you need to know about the English.

Today Anna and Katerina, two of the palace maids, came to change my stinking sheets. As they came up the stairs they were laughing as if at something indecent, and I made out my brother's name. But by the time they got to the door of my room they were discussing my father.

'My husband says it's a ploy,' said Anna. 'Milosh is buying time. His supporters are coming together in the forests and soon they will march on Belgrade and he will be there to meet them. No one wants the regency, everyone knows those three are just Turkish puppets.'

'What does your husand know?' said Katerina, helping Anna to lift me on to the divan by the window. I kept my eyes shut and my limbs limp. They were wasting their time: in a few hours, the clean sheets they put on the bed would be, as usual, already so sodden with my sweat and blood and bile as to be indistinguishable from the old ones.

'Everyone is saying so. Milosh would not give up so easily.'

'I hate Milosh.'

'So does everyone. But we love him, too.'

Later, Michael came in while Cuniberto was attending to me. Cuniberto makes me drink bowls of bitter boiled herbs, which I take great pleasure in slopping out of my mouth into his lap like a baby. Hippocrates warned physicians to refuse to treat patients with consumption, because there is no hope of curing them, but Cuniberto is too stupid to realise that. The peasants in the north will try to cure an outbreak of the white plague by digging up whoever was first to die of it and burning their heart. I'd rather have them treating me than Cuniberto, even though it's said many of them are born with tails. I once spat in Cuniberto's eye in an attempt to pass on my disease but it doesn't seem to have worked.

When Michael came in he asked Cuniberto about my condition and my medicines and so on, but paced around and did not listen to the physician's responses. Finally, irritated, he motioned at Cuniberto to shut up, and revealed his real purpose. 'Do you know anything about poisons?' he said.

'A little,' said Cuniberto. His Italian accent makes him sound like a catamite. Meanwhile Michael's voice hasn't properly broken yet, so it's difficult to take seriously anything that either of them says. 'What do you wish to know?'

'What is the most lethal poison?'

'In China there is a sort of lotus which can, with a handful of its pollen, kill a whole regiment of - '

'I mean, what is the most lethal poison we have in Serbia?'

'Arsenic, strychnine, hemlock, foxglove, certain mushrooms ... They will all kill.'

'How does one get hold of these poisons?'

'Perhaps from an apothecary. They know how to prepare them properly.'

'Aren't you an apothecary?' demanded Michael.

'Yes. But my business is not murder.'

Michael went out, grumbling under his breath. The last thing I heard him say was, 'One day everyone will get what they deserve.'

Now Cuniberto has gone and I lie wondering about Michael. He must have heard the rumours - ludicrous, in my opinion - that the Maggot is going to make a triumphant return to the throne. My brother was expecting to be Prince by the end of the summer, and may not be willing to resign himself to another long wait. Perhaps he intends to 'get what he deserves': the crown. Is my brother plotting to assassinate our father? If so, I can hardly believe he is on his own. He can barely piss without aid. Is he in league with our uncle Jevrem?

With that thug Vutchich? With the Whore? But if so, why is he making such idiotic and indiscrete queries to Cuniberto? I couldn't care less what happens to my father, but I would be interested to know what is going on in this palace.

This morning the Whore paid me another visit, dragging my brother with her. I had no interest in talking to them so I pretended to be unconscious. My mother fussed over me pointlessly for a few minutes, then went off, followed by Michael. As they left, Anna and Katerina came in. My mother stopped for a moment in the doorway to talk to Katerina - her favourite maid - about supper, but I could see that Katerina was finding it hard to concentrate because Michael, who stood behind my mother, was staring at her with an expression of volcanic rage. Then when my mother went down the stairs my brother took Katerina by the shoulder and slammed her savagely against the jamb of the door before spitting at her feet and going down after the Princess. Anna exchanged a glance with Katerina that I could not interpret, and then they began to sweep the room.

Before today I have only seen my brother's face so reddened and contorted with anger when he's been badly humiliated. Once, when we were both very young, Michael refused to get into his bath so his nursemaid carried him, still naked, to see our father, who was with his advisers. Then there was the occasion at the High School when Isailovic joked about Michael's intelligence in front of the whole class. Worst of all was the time my father decided my brother's stealing had gone far enough, stormed into our (as it was then) shared bedroom, pulled down Michael's breeches, and thrashed his goosepimpled arse with a cane. What could Katerina have down to inspire equivalent hatred? I could only conclude that my brother had tried to get her into bed and she'd had the courage to refuse him. She has a face like a hanged man, but she does have big heaving tits, which Michael has always liked. I decided to investigate as best I could.

When Anna and Katerina had finished sweeping, I pretended to wake up. 'Katerina,' I whispered. She came over to my bedside. 'Katerina, my brother has borrowed a folio from me and I'd like it back. Could you get it from his room?'

'Um, I'm afraid I can't, Your Highness. Yesterday morning your brother forbid me from going into his room ever again without his specific permission.'

'Tell me, why is that?' I said. Katerina and Anna looked at each other and then burst out laughing. Quickly they stifled their giggles and Katerina tried to compose a response, but I'd already closed my eyes and rolled over, and soon after that they left the room.

There was something in the mocking tone of their laughter which makes me certain I was wrong before. Michael didn't try for a fuck and get turned down - it was something even more ridiculous and bathetic. The probable truth, I now realise, is this: Michael was lying in bed, sheet thrown back, throttling his grotesque stub of a penis, breathlessly enjoying himself for no doubt already the second or third time that day, imagining - who knows? - his face between Katerina's tits, or our mother hauling herself out of the bath, or the time our father caned him, when Katerina came in without knocking and caught him in the act - seeing, before she blushed and ran out, something that no mortal creature should ever have to see.

An embarrassment of that magnitude is not something my brother would forget in a hurry. Could it be that my father is not the real target of his murderous intentions? Could it be poor Katerina instead who is to 'get what she deserves'? Normally, if he wanted, he could have any of the palace's servants flogged and then dismissed for whatever transgression he decided to invent, but Katerina is my mother's favourite maid; the Princess would never allow my brother to do her wrong. So he's planning to kill her. He's on his way to becoming one of the great men of Serbia. My father would be delighted if he knew.

When the Whore came in today I said to her, 'I would like you to dismiss Katerina.'

'What on earth makes you say that?' she said.

'She's lazy. Careless. Disrespectful.'

'That's nonsense, Milan. I won't get rid of my best maid just because you don't like her. Your father's gone now and - what I mean is, until your father gets back, we won't be like that to our servants.' My father used to treat his private secretaries worse than he treated his livestock.

'I insist, mother.'

'I won't have it. But if you like, I'll make sure she doesn't come in here any more.'

Then I would have no more chances to save her, I thought. My father dying as the result of a secret coup is one thing - that's the least the Maggot deserves. But I wouldn't stain my last week on this earth by letting my brother murder an innocent girl. 'No. She's better than the others at changing the sheets.'

'I thought you said she was careless?'

I hesitated. 'Mother, Katerina is in danger.'

She looked concerned, but probably more for my mind than her maid. 'From whom?'

'Michael.'

'Milan, no one is in danger from Michael. He's just a little boy. You're delirious.'

I faked a coughing fit and she went off to look for Cuniberto.

Later, Anna and Katerina came in to change my sheets. When they'd finished I said to Katerina, 'You must leave the palace.' She ignored me. 'My brother wants to kill you.' Her eyes flicked towards me but she still didn't answer. 'Listen, you witless peasant, if you don't want to die then go home and don't come back!' I tried to shout but my scabby throat wouldn't allow more than a hoarse bark.

'We can't go home, Your Highness,' said Anna softly. 'We have children to feed.'

This morning the Whore came in with my uncle Jevrem. As usual I feigned sleep, keeping one eye just a little open so I could watch them.

'Shall we wake him?' Jevrem said. He wore a turban.

'Why?' said my mother. 'We will just have to tell him a lot of lies.'

Jevrem chuckled. 'You don't care about telling him lies. You just can't wait to get my cock in your mouth.'

I made a noise, somewhere between a mumble and a moan, and jerked my shoulders. I have found that the best way to make people confident that you can't hear them is not to keep silent - that's what eavesdroppers do - but to pretend you're deep in a fever-dream.

'You're a pig,' said my mother.

'Let's do it now,' said Jevrem, grabbing her between her legs. My mother squealed and slapped his hand away.

'We can't,' she said. 'The maids will be coming in to sweep the room.'

'I'll have them too.'

'I thought you wanted to speak to him.'

'I do. We musn't neglect our pale Prince. Wake him up.'

My mother shook my shoulder, and I pretended to wake. Jevrem bent as if to kiss my forehead but then thought better of it. 'Do you feel any better, nephew?' he said.

'A little,' I replied. This was a lie: already I could feel my strength draining away like scummy bath-water. 'Tell me, uncle, do you know when my father will be coming back? No one seems to be quite sure.'

Jevrem started to stutter something, but my mother intervened, just as she had with my brother. 'You're tired, Milan. We should let you rest. Say goodbye to your uncle.' I did so, happy in the knowledge that it was the last time I would ever see him.

Half an hour later my brother came in holding an axe.

'Where's that bitch?' he shouted. He had obviously given up on poison.

'Who?' I said.

'The maid with the ugly face. Katerina.'

'What do you want with her?'

'Where is she? She's meant to be here.'

'The maids have already come in.' My brother could have exposed my lie with one sniff of my sheets, which hadn't been changed for two days, but that didn't occur to him.

'Where are they now?'

'In the kitchens, I think. Or the gardens.'

He left. I lay in bed, staring at the ceiling, hoping Katerina wouldn't be unlucky enough to meet him on the stairs. A few minutes later I was relieved to see her and Anna come in. This time there wasn't time to wait for them to finish their duties, in case Michael returned.

'Katerina, get my mother,' I said.

'Your Highness, the Princess said she was not to be disturbed.'

'It's important.'

'She was very clear, Your Highness...' said Katerina, fiddling with a loose thread on her apron, not sure what to do.

'I'm dying, Katerina. I may only have a few more moments of life. I must see her.'

She had a short whispered conversation with Anna which I couldn't quite hear. Then she said, 'All right, Your Highness,' and left the room unhappily. Katerina looked at me with reproach. I could not tell her that, if I'd had the strength, I would have taken the axe from Michael and beaten him to the brink of death, or, if my sovereignty had been acknowledged, I would have made duchesses of my two maids.

A minute later I could hear the angry shouts of my mother from downstairs. Then Katerina came back up, sobbing. 'She will not come. I opened the door and she was... with your uncle. She says I'm to leave the palace and not come back.' This last news was directed less at me than at Anna, who burst into tears herself and embraced Katerina. 'What will I do for my daughter?' wailed Katerina. 'I have no husband! Why am I cursed always to open the wrong door?'

'Katerina,' I said. She looked down at me resentfully. 'Look in the chest at the foot of the bed.'

'I'm not your maid any more!' she said.

'Just look in it.' She did so. 'Take all the money in there,' I said. 'For your daughter.'

'I cannot, Your Highness,' she said.

'Take them. You've already lost your job. And they're certainly no use to me any more. Share them with Anna if you like.'

Again, the two maids whispered to each other, then Anna went away and came back with a cloth sack. They knelt down. I was too weak to sit up and see but I could hear them filling the sack with the silver dinars from the chest.

Katerina came over and kissed me on the forehead. I could feel her tears where her cheek brushed my face. 'Thank you, Your Highness,' she said.

'Leave quickly, or my mother will be angry.'

Katerina said goodbye to Anna, and then went away. Anna started to tidy the room. A few minutes later my brother came in, still carrying his axe, his knuckles white on the wooden handle.

'You!' he roared at Anna. 'Where is your little slut friend? I've searched everywhere.'

'The Princess sent her away,' Anna replied.

My brother stepped forward and slapped Anna across the face. 'Bitch!' Then he stamped over to me. For a moment I thought he was about raise the axe and split me in half as if I was a log. 'I'm to be king, you know! Our father is in exile! They haven't told you because you're such a fucking ugly weakling!'

'I know all that, Michael,' I said quietly. 'I may be a weakling but I'm not an idiot.'

Michael spat at me - he missed as usual - and left. Anna knelt on the floor, crying.

'You can go now, Anna.' She didn't move. 'Did you hear me? Please go.'

She went out. That was a few minutes ago. The funny thing is that I wasn't lying to Katerina when I told her that I didn't have long to live. I'm gasping air now but it still feels as if I'm drowning. I'm losing feeling in my arms and legs. My vision is darkening like the evening sky. I have little to be proud of in this life but I'm proud of saving Katerina. I can see her now, running home to her daughter - and I can see my brother, wandering around with my axe, looking for something to destroy - and I can see the Whore, the whole incident already forgotten, climbing once again on top of my uncle - and I can see the Maggot across the river, bored now that he has no one to put to death - and I can see him in the future, King again, somehow - and I can see Serbia - my domain - its villages - its Turks and gypsies and Jews and Greeks and Vlachs and Bulgars - its bandits and wolves in the forest, its thieves and dogs in the towns - outlaws swinging from gibbets or dangling on wheels by the roads - and I see the years pass - horror and calamity and farce - rifles piled upon rifles - balls of fire - bitter smoke - murder made efficient - all this I see in Serbia's future - I see that its great men do not learn mercy - and I see, beyond doubt now, that God is no more real than the crooked bishop from Kragujevac - I see that I have nothing to look forward to - and I see that, unlike my ungrateful subjects, I have nothing to fear.

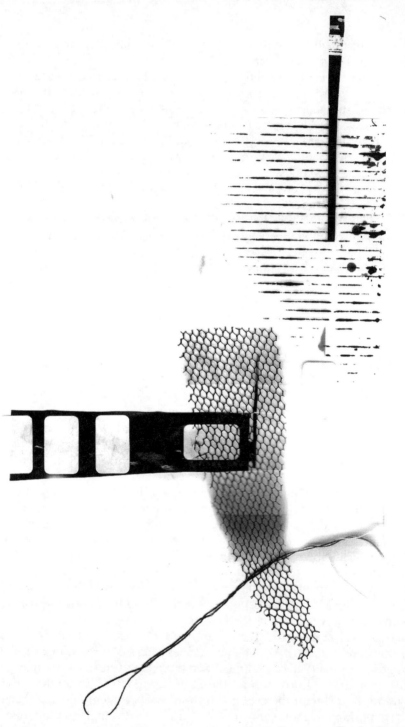

Pooja Agrawal

Ted Hodgkinson

The Pillowcase

Guck feels like his stomach has already been buried for a week. The worms teem down his piping hot piping and drop through the translucent air. The desert spits suns in his eyes. They close - irritated oysters full of angry pearls that boil and fizz down the sides of his face like white peas. Guck's lids are flaky with dry skin and missing people. The wind is unforgivable. Guck's favourite ointment for raw eyes is his father's tape measure. Guck's father could make a box for anything with that tape measure. Guck doubts that the towel heads made a box for him. Guck thinks that maybe part of the black smoke that fills the sky was burnt off his Dad's sides. Alright, haunches. He had haunches. They probably incinerated him, ate his toenails and teeth. Yep.

Guck remembers the pillowcase that he hid between his mattress and the bed frame. He hid it there because he got blood on it. He didn't want anyone to know why and he still don't. Guck cut his cock. He got it caught on his watch and it bled like a brain. He soaked it all up with his pillowcase and hid it there for all time, as ever. Now he's sitting in a truck in a military convoy in the desert thinking about it. God. Guck picks a scab on his thick forearm. It cries. Guck dabs it and tastes it. It tastes of women, sanctitude and wrath. Sometimes when Guck couldn't sleep he'd take out that pillowcase and put his pillow in it and sleep with his head on the dried blood. He fancied it looked like a map of the world. Guck slept better with that pillowcase on. Guck guesses how many grains of sand there are in the desert and gets it wrong by forty seven trillion and six. Guck thinks about all the bits of wallpaper that got ripped off his bedroom wall when he took his posters down. That's like the world, he thinks.

Once, in the morning a bat flew into Guck's room. He'd been sleeping on his bloody pillowcase – the map of the world one. He woke up with this black armpit flapping in his face so he swung his pillow at the witchcraft and it stuck to the wall like a hairy eye. Guck watched it peel off and die on the floor. Guck looks up at the faces, they don't look like looking back. The guy on his right places his right index finger to his right nostril and blows snot on Guck's jacket and face. Guck twists like a broken axle but does nothing because that guy and his snot have got guts enough to die gagged and bagged next to him. And because he doesn't want to die gagged and bagged next to him. Guck doesn't want anyone to see the piss stains on his trousers until they get fighting, then he'll be a man that pissed himself for his country. Guck had a fight with his English teacher once. Guck liked English, he liked stories, they felt nice. This guy, this guy, this guy was saying something about war and futility well he must have known, he must have known, he, known, must. Guck hit him with the staple gun and one came out stapling his cheek to his jawbone, like futility. Guck's dad died for his country. Guck's family died for their country. Guck is dying for cunt. He drains his water bottle, like he's sucking a black cloud teat.

A helicopter beats its wings like a harpy over head and carves holes in the sky such as you might find in the centre of a doughnut or between a woman's legs. Guck rubs his teeth and curls his toes. Guck wonders what God is doing right now. If God is everywhere and knows everything that means God just thought that, and that and that and that. Take that and that and that and that you coward son of a bitch! Guck wants God to know he didn't think that. God knows that already. Guck doesn't understand why he doesn't understand when so many other people seem to. His mum understands. She loves understanding. She breast-fed him her milk. Guck's mother keeps his milk-teeth and toe-nails in a box Guck's father made. She knows about the pillowcase. She wants to wash it. Have it tested for drugs. A nose-bleed?

They roll through the desert. A frown on the horizon, a cordon that circles everyone. Guck has a lump in his throat. He shot a bear once with a lump of a similar size but this one was made of lead. It was in Alaska with his dad. What a peach of a shot. This old man said the Alaskan Indians or Inuit (whatever the fuck) used to call bears "That Which Went Away," or so the guy at the petrol pump told them. Guck didn't know what to make of this. Guck remembers his last night with Jodie. She's on top bouncing around on his cock and it just goes soft. Guck can't explain it, he laughs, he feels relieved. Jodie is pissed. Guck suddenly wants it but she wont touch him. It's too late she says, the moment's gone.

The bolts on the truck jolt and jilt like a rickety sex life. Guck wants his pillowcase. Guck thinks about the towel head he saw a mile back, his face like a stolen leather handbag, his eyes like a ladies stolen earrings. The landscape looks like a fire in an art gallery. Paint turning back into oil.

The trucks grind to a halt. A noise like a wall falling on a house. The air is brash and addictive, the soil is quaking like a custard skin.

Radios crackle and pop. Voices command the voiceless. Boots grace metal boards and then the dust of the world's carpet. War is come. Three rockets that seem to be dripping with blood scream past their helmets and rifle down thousands. Atoms split up for good. Machine guns dribbling spittle through the air like the whole army is firing from behind a diamond beaded doorway. Troops swarm like insects and parasites running across the dunes like iron filings being lead by a magnet that is nowhere to be seen. A black bird sees it all until it is dashed on the windscreen of the sky by an anti-aircraft shell.

War excites the genitals. One soldier's erection is so hard he can't run properly. One soldier can't stop thinking about the other one's erection. Another one vomits on to his hand and his rifle. A bullet glances off a pair of glasses and into a stomach. A piece of bombshell severs an ear and it lands in someone's pocket. Cinders fill the air as if the day had been heated up on a bonfire.

Guck runs. Guck's teeth are gritted so hard they are chipping like china plates at a fair. The world is a kid with fireworks in its pockets. Guck swings his pillowcase and beats the towel heads down. He brings the heavy sack of feathers around the front of a face that shatters like one of his mum's special vases. Guck swipes at them and brings them down to the monstrous floor. I'll teach you, I'll teach you, I'll teach you. Guck thinks about all the things that make no sense to him as he swings the pillowcase (riddled with tears and bullet holes) feathers begin to shower around him in a soft confetti. Guck doesn't understand why we have to have full stops in sentences, what he should think about the President, where bullets go when they die, why no one listens to him, why no one else has a pillowcase? This last question makes Guck stop. Why is he the only one fighting with a pillow instead of a gun? He looks up and to his relief he realises he is not the only one. A guy over there, that one with the blood on his teeth and the flame thrower canister on his back, he's racking skull with a heavy duck down pillow in a homey blue checked case. It smells of fabric softener and his mother, he keeps his porn mag in it. Guck sees two more pillows lilting above the death like boys in a choppy ocean. Suddenly Guck is hit in the back, a dull soft thud. Guck turns around expecting to find half his back on the floor but instead finds a towel-head swinging a pillow for a return blow. Guck raises his pillowcase to hit back, harder. There is still violence.

Owen Holland

Jonathan Birch

Care

He sits on the tram, agitated. Across the aisle in the next-but-one seat the madwoman spews invective, as though it were the script to some long-forgotten soap opera.

"Go away you stupid Middleton cunt. At least I'm not a murderer like Andrea."

He watches as a group of boys (lad, yob, chav shoot through his head like darts, a piercing trio, one hundred and eighty) stand up and move closer. Each new torrent they parry with hollow taunts and a wall of laughter, egging-on:

"Andrea's a murderer then?"

"Who did she kill?"

He does not find it so simple to shield himself from this madwoman's abuse. It is radial, without vector: Andrea is not present. But it hits him indiscriminately, like noise and heat and light. Is this news important? Perhaps, for the greater good of public safety, he should run to the local police station to report the secret crime. "It was Andrea!" he will proclaim. "I have a witness!"

More likely, surely, that the murder has no tangible reality, no forensics, no fingerprints, nothing to sign and date and file. It did not happen. But a murder exists in the memory of the madwoman, that much is evident. The murder is an idea. An idea spawned of dementia? The dementia itself is not contagious, but its spawn has apparently infected him.

Murderer like Andrea murderer like Andrea murderer like go away cunt murder go away Middleton like murder Andrea Andrea and it as though the dementia has become his. Where is Mr. Andrea, Prime Suspect?

The boys still laugh. He considers: what disease, what symptom is to blame for this? Has the madwoman relived the lonely rages of Beethoven? Improbable: for some unfathomable reason he sees the madwoman as something closer to an aged Sylvia Plath. There is a peculiar poetry to her raving.

"You can't get away. You don't just speak to me like this. I'll get you in the fucking back, in the back. You're all the same. All the same I said. Piss off."

He admires the perfect irony with which the madwoman's faculties have been trimmed. The vocabulary, the correct tram stop, the mobility (she holds a flimsy little stick) are all in tact. He could well imagine spending his last days as a disabled intellectual: lost, lame and inwardly philosophising. But this is something quite opposite.

It must start with something small. Were such a thing to strike him, would he ever know? The first clue would be an unusual prescription. "It's your seratonin, Sir, you needn't worry." Diseased brains happen all the time.

Then the little lapses: Where are my keys? It's Friday already? No longer bipolar disorder, the magnificent euphemism usurped by something altogether more blunt. Schizophrenia. Alzheimer's. He pities poor Alzheimer: how could the man have known the terror his name would inspire? Perhaps Alzheimer ought to have been shrewder, like Nobel. He has always felt that a legacy has a life quite separate to its parent: a life greater or lesser or stillborn.

Of course, maybe the madwoman even now does not know. To the madwoman, this crowd of taciturn business suits and cackling boys must seem demented indeed; they offer no cogent reply. He and his crowd must be ghosts and demons in the eyes of the madwoman.

This is the madwoman's Principia Matematica, and Ode to Joy, and Ariel, and no one is listening.

"Oi! It's been fifty years I've had that bicycle I never thought I'd see the day. I can't move for the dickheads. They run the company. They fucking run every fucking company. England for the English that's what I say, England for the English."

For a moment he wishes the flow were severed, with a rush of fluoxetine, or diamorphine or coal fumes. Stop these ideas, don't let them spread, the madwoman is an embarrassment. An embarrassment above all else to the medical profession. If this cannot be cured, how can he feel safe? For his sake this ought to end.

He must escape. He must exorcise Andrea from his vulnerable mind.

—

At the next stop he walks away from the tram. The boys follow. But they walk quietly and keep a respectful distance; perhaps their conformity to the yob form is not so complete. He feels faintly sorry for them, sorry for their indifference. A boy throws to one side half a burger in cheap polystyrene casing. The inelegant word nonbiodegradable slips and skids through his head.

He pictures the odd specimen a thousand years later, pored over by some three-eyed archaeologist:

> This custom followed the sacrifice of animals, the rite of cfcfree. The flesh was burned and compressed into a disc so as to be unrecognisable, transubstantiated. Swathed in vegetable and bread and plastic it could then be consumed.

And this, in the fantasy, is the boy's legacy. He permits himself a sardonic smile. But he can imagine worse fates.

He would settle for an uncomplicated little gift to posterity. Better than nothing. Better than the chance products of a volatile mind, thrown out into the world like noise and heat and light. He will rot. And he asks himself what will be left, what will live on, after the degradation.

—

Minutes later and, as he stands fumbling for a key at his front door, and unwelcome sight drifts into view. He spies the madwoman inching steadily along the pavement, fifty yards distant. Of the sky he asks: What trick of fate is this? What invisible puppeteer contrived this hideous rendezvous?

Distracted from the task at hand, he once more tries the lock with the wrong key. It jams and he wrests the key loose. Before the door is opened the madwoman stands at the gate of the driveway.

To his surprise, the madwoman is silent. Her breath is spent on the exertion of hobbling. She stops, rests on her stick and then, in small increments, turns to face him. To his disgust, he is relieved she is not more mobile.

"Excuse me," she says and a shiver runs down his back, accompanied by a rush of shame. He looks into a pair of eyes lined with bags of sickly deep grey. "Where is my house?"

His stomach crawls; he suppresses an impulse to contort into a cringe. The sensation is akin to drowning: his mind flails in search of a life raft response; he chokes on every word.

"I.
"I don't.
"Would you like me to call?" (Who?)
"Come in."

He hopes that she does not understand. But, grasping her stick firmly, the madwoman begins to walk towards him. He opens the door, leads to a chair and gestures that she may sit. She sits.

"I will make tea," he says, and walks away. What one ought to do, he thinks, is phone one's friend the social worker. But his friends are lawyers, journalists and executives in various fields. Who else is there? There seems scant justification for an ambulance. Calling the police again occurs to him, this time with some sly fiction: "I think she saw a murder! Someone called Andrea!" But he has always struggled with the practicalities of dishonesty. The lie would not come naturally to him.

Buried in the website of the local council is an emergency duty number. He dials immediately; he has quite forgotten about tea. When prompted, he gives an eloquent summary:

"There is a madwoman in my house. She has lost her mind and now she has lost her bearings."

On the other end of the line the woman pauses, perhaps sighs inaudibly.
"Is she a danger to herself and/or others?"

"What?" He realises the correct answer is Yes. "I think so," he says awkwardly. He wonders how many calls of this type the woman handles. He gives contact details and is told to hang up while his case is passed to the duty social worker. He has no idea how they deal with such matters. The phone could ring in five minutes. It may not ring for hours.

The madwoman still sits rigid on the chair as if frozen. He lowers himself on to a piano stool and they sit in silence. After a minute:

"I don't have time to waste on the likes of you you dickhead mechanic. They don't argue when they get lockjaw. Lord Finch wouldn't spit on your fucking feet. Who do you think you are? When I was your age I…"

It is monotone, flowing, unthreatening.

"Stop," he says.

"… think you're so good working in the kitchen. One day I'll knife you. Knife your fucking family Maureen. You deserve a dead cat in my back yard, I said…"

Without exception the stories are facile and illiterate. What is it he finds so disturbing? Like all citizens he is trained to let the noise of society wash over him, yet this noise catches and sticks like needles in his skin. And it is all the more painful, now he is the only audience. He and this madwoman, this (he is reluctant to think the word) subhuman are linked by some new and vile connection, a connection that brings no understanding to either participant.

"Stop! STOP!"

"What? Where is my house?"

And now the pathetic lost soul returns and he cannot tell which is worse, which is the more tormenting company. The absence of purpose envelops her whole divided being in a repulsive darkness. Nothing the madwoman does can break through to the cool light of human recognition. No one answers her questions; everyone wants to shut the door. And he, of all people, wants to shut her out more than anyone.

But, for a few minutes or a few hours, he has to care.

"Tell me what you remember," he says. "Say what you can, and I will write down what you say."

Paul Castro

James Knight

The Dead

The wet smacks of their blows resounded off each of the three walls, the dull fleshy thuds of their palms and the leather ball muted in the soft Dublin gloom. Cosgrave's back, beaded with mist and sweat, bobbed idly while Byrne, thickset but athletic, lunged at the front of the court, his excited cries strangely distant as they bounced around the blind alley.

Thomas Kettle watched the game restlessly, shifting his weight in reflection of his friends' exertions, his movements rocking the crate on which stocky Frank Skeffington, in his plus fours, peacefully reclined. Behind them George Clancy stood earnestly watching, his brow furrowed in concentration, occasionally turning to observe the tall, disinterested form of James Joyce.

—Do you not see the majesty of the game though, Jim?

Clancy's rustic voice rose chimingly to James' ears and he couldn't prevent a smile from cracking his gaunt lips. What he saw was Byrne stooping to pick up the ball from the mudscuppered ground before propelling it from his hand to the far corner of the court. Cranly's arm. His arm.

Skeffington's voice issued from his Cavalier beard as his body still reposed.

—Joyce has no need to see majesty for he is king of his realm.

—He can't be the King, chimed Clancy, that's a German fella, goes by the handle of Ed, you must have heard of him.

—Englishman, German, Orangeman, tinkerman, muttered Kettle.

—I meant, proceeded Skeffington, that Joyce is king in his own mind and has no need of any greater country.

James smiled more broadly, his cheeks creasing deeply as he contemplated his three friends and the nation they loved but which existed only in their minds.

—Thank you, Skeff, he replied.

—It was not entirely intended as a compliment, said Skeffington, turning his neck away from the game to face James.

—Be thy intents wicked or charitable, smiled the tall student, thou com'st in such a questionable shape, that I will speak to thee.

—You do me great service, mugged Skeffington.

—Hamlet, declared Clancy, was too stout for handball. You, Jim, are too lean. These sports will mould the body of the Irish race, just as our language will mould its soul. Do you not think, Jim?

James was silent.

Another rally ended with the ball on the wet ground. Kettle turned to join the conversation.

—What happened to those Irish classes you were going to, Joyce?

Clancy waited for James to answer, then filled the silence with his explanation.

—He did not share Pearse's disdain for the language of our rulers.

—Patrick Pearse has 'arse' in his name for a reason, snapped James. If he can't hear the beauty of the word thunder he must be deaf to the thunder itself.

Into early adolescence James had felt the terror of death in thunderstorms. As the rain pounded the darkstaring windows his smothering mother would pull down the blinds and draw the curtains whilst he hid in the cupboard. He would not have the thunderword abused.

As mist turned to fine rain the ball dropped again, rolling to a halt near the feet of two girls approaching from the direction of the University. Skeffington's eyes followed Hanna Sheehy's measured steps as they rippled her long brown skirt. Hanna's sister Mary's silken rope of deep brown hair flicked against her breasts, entrancing Kettle as she bent her knees to pick up the little muddied globe, lifting the hem of her skirt out of the slush a little with her other hand. As she straightened again and tossed the ball back to the sweat-drenched players, her neat figure was silhouetted by the dull light of a newly lit gas lamp behind her. The sisters passed the spectators with furtive greetings met by muttered acknowledgements. James watched the back of Mary's head silently as the girls receded into the encircling gloom.

Clancy observed his companions with a wry smile.

—I think we can all agree, he said, that there are some things of which this country can justly be proud.

James continued to gaze into the murmurous murderous mist for a calm second before turning back to his innocent friend.

—But she herself is not so sweet, he said. She suffocates those she suckles.

—Oh, very neat, said Skeffington, like all your choice little phrases, but for all the bloodshed and brutality of our past, you surely cannot discount the simple beauty of our art, of the ballads you are so fond…

—O come all you Firbolgs that will not fight for Erin, sang James in the full voice which gave his words more venom than he intended.

Kettle looked disdainfully at the singing youth and said sharply:

—Maybe Skeff's vegetarian, teetotal, feminist pacifism won't let him fight for ourselves, but I will. I would die for Ireland.

James turned to face the assault.

—I say, let Ireland die for me.

Clancy looked, soft and broken, at the man he so admired, and said in his simple accent:

—You mean it, don't you, Jim? You are so fascinated and repulsed by our land that you would murder it in order to dissect it. You so long to preserve its paralysing force that you would paralyse it yourself.

James stood, staring at the handball game, lost.

Silence ruled the four friends as they stood at the crossroads and each saw the path before him. Kettle inclined his head in the muttering rain: his ears seemed lost to a distant music.

Coming back he said softly to James:

—While you make pretty speeches we're being cut to shreds.

—We're pushing up the daisies whilst you are in Bloom, Skeffington added in his lightly mocking tone.

Clancy's lilting voice joined the chorus:

—You are Dedalus. We are the dead.

James looked rapidly from one friend to another, searching their earnest faces for some hint of what they meant. Were they saying these things for cod? Why did they stare that way? The gloaming dusk closed in around them.

Kettle again broke the silence.

—In two years' time you leave Ireland for the continent, a self-enforced exile. Free from the hemiplegia of Dublin, you write a great many things and many great things. You write about the life you leave behind you. You write about us.

The searing taste of bile darted through James' throat. In weak defiance he said:

—You are right to go your way. Leave me to go mine.

—You long to escape the world around you, to record it and thus step outside of it, an impartial observer. But the world does not let you escape. Europe is gripped by war and, while you are surrounded by tormenting tragedies and the agonies of the soul, you write the tragedy of the bedroom.

Skeffington's voice full of wit interrupted.

—Our dear Stephen Hero is more concerned with *Wilhelm Meister* than with Kaiser Wilhelm.

James was silent. Clancy told him simply:

—In the time that you are writing your greatest work we are all killed.

Skeffington's eyelashes were bejewelled with tears and the raindrops.

—In April 1916, he said in a still voice, you are in Zurich when Padraig Pearse, the very man whose language classes you attended and abandoned, leads his Irish Republican Brotherhood, along with James Connolly's Sinn Féin, in what is known as the Easter Rising. Your beloved streets of Dublin are once again home to bloodshed. The General Post Office is taken before the English regain forceful control of the city run amok. I, in my pacifistic optimism, take to the streets to discourage my countrymen from looting, and, as I return home on the evening of Tuesday, April 25th, am arrested by members of the 11th East Surrey Regiment. Though I survived a hunger strike when previously arrested for speaking out against conscription of Irishmen for the British forces, I am not so resilient this time around. Upon the orders of a Captain Bowen-Colthurst, who is soon after declared insane, I am shot without charge the following morning at dawn. My wife, Hanna Sheehy-Skeffington, lives on without me until 1946.

James' soul reeled with the resounding blast in his head as he saw his friend shot to bloody bits with a bang shotgun, bits man spattered walls all brass buttons. Bits all khrrrklak in place clack back. Zurich. It was not his fault. It was not. His eyes rolled to Kettle, whose calm stare stilled them. Kettle's lips began to speak.

—I make my own trip to Europe in 1914, one month before the outbreak of the Great War. I am sent to Belgium to procure arms for ourselves, but have my intentions changed when Britain decides to fight for that small nation against German atrocities. I think that, if we help in this noble endeavour, the gratitude of Britain will make her equally generous to our small nation. I return to Ireland, enlist in the Royal Dublin Fusiliers, and speak at enlistment rallies across the country.

Kettle paused, smiling gently through James' confusion. The handball game continued in the muted rain. The smile descended into a remorseful grimace and Kettle continued:

—The Easter Rising and Frank's death leave me disillusioned and depressed. The years to come seem waste of breath. I request to fight in France, leaving Mary behind me, and find myself in the heart of the Somme Offensive. On 9th September 1916, my Division conducts an assault on the German held village of Ginchy. The British bombardment of German defences before the assault is ineffective as the mortar shells fall short, only churning the mud of no-man's land, and, though the attack is successful in taking the village, many Irish lives are lost. My body is never recovered and lies in the blood-soaked clay, pecked at by birds while my flesh decays in the rain.

James looked down at the sullen mud and saw only the prophetic clay. An Irish infantryman foresees his death.

—I make it a little farther, Jim, said Clancy kindly. I even get to become Lord Mayor of Limerick. My ardent support of the Gaelic League and the Gaelic Athletic Association is put to good use, but is not universally appreciated. On the night of March 6th 1921, as you work on the final stages of *Ulysses* in Paris, two auxiliaries of the infamous British regiment, the Black and Tans, force entry to my comfortable house. They are not acting upon any orders and have, like myself, a drop taken. You always told me that drink was the quickest way to the devil, and I believe you were right. I confront them in the front hall, my wife hurrying downstairs behind me but unable to do more than shiver in her nightdress at the foot of the stairs. As I approach the two intruders they grab an arm each and subdue me with embarrassing ease. One of them then holds both my arms in a lock behind my back while the other pulls out a military issue blade. As he approaches me slowly all I see is my wife, quivering in the cold, sweat from her forehead mingling with tears on her frozen cheeks. My hot blood arcs as I fall and it continues to issue from my neck as I lie, flowing slowly along the grain of the wooden floor, collecting in winedark pools around my throat."

James stood silent. Eyes aghast he stared at the shaded faces. Clancy spoke again:

—You needn't worry though, Jim. You're not here.

—You scut off to Rome, Trieste, Zurich, Paris, added Kettle.

—In 1922, said Skeffington, you attend a dinner in Paris with Stravinsky, Picasso, and Proust. Conversation is strained. Proust spends the evening complaining about his stomach ache and wishing you would go away.

—But you do attend his funeral, noted Clancy. We don't expect you to attend ours.

James could take it no longer, the jibes of the prophets riled him into desperation.

—Why are you telling me this? His knees were weak as he

implored them. What is my crime? Do you condemn me because I am not to die in some war?

—Oh, you die in a war, alright, said Skeffington.

—In occupied France, in 1941, added Kettle.

—From a perforated stomach ulcer, said Clancy. Half blind and bloated.

James again looked at the ground.

—But in many ways, said Kettle, you cannot die. You are preserved in your books. Each gumbound page, each polished period, each 'f', broken in type, is your monument. You imprison yourself in Dublin in a million black vertical lines, and so you cannot die.

—One of the Invincibles, joked Skeffington.

Clancy smiled his warming smile at his perplexed friend.

—Your words will always linger on beyond our simple instants of death, he said, for language speaks longer than reticent fact. What you find and record in reference and poetry and music we can look for only in death.

Skeffington nodded his assent.

—We live in dark and evil days, he said, and your voice will speak of them long after we have faded with the dying sunlight.

—Darkness falls from the air, said Kettle.

The game had stopped. Long ago the light had failed and now the players sloped away. James' thoughts went with them, away from here. His soul flowed down the Liffey, and out into the sea. But each wave bore him back, breaking upon the shore again and again. Each thought dissolved into thin white foam, lapping the gravel at Howth, sucking his homeland stones as they receded.

The gloaming embraced them as the cold rain descended, and night was falling softly, softly falling upon all the living and the dead.

Ciaran O'Conaill

Mechanical Piece for Unfinished Piano

My aunt died last week.

   My father was in the middle of changing a lightbulb when the phonecall came; & afterwards he couldn't stand, his sister dead, & the empty socket hanging there like a broken thing, blind & inconsolable.

   At the removal, the priest anointed her head with holy water, just here, above her eyebrows; & the water ran slowly down, down around the hollow about her eye & down the side of her cheek; & there came to me, just at that moment, & very clearly, an image of her – there was snow on the ground & a rancid smell of burning in the air; & she lay there quite still, her eyes closed & her hands folded, as her tears fell & cut the snow.

Citystreamnoise & darkening light through the open window.

   Time collects on your dusky skin & under my hands that are on you; & I can feel, moving, under your skin, (& this movement I will carry with me now, as part of me), the gentle breathing of the air.

   There are moments of incandescence, when I would like to cry for happiness. (These are usually with her.)

   & moments of serenity too, sitting at my desk, when it is covered in sunlight, wrapped in it, & there is a glare from the sheets (which seem somehow to be more solid, & almost with a kind of depth), & my hands are warm – the sun warming my blood.

   And yet there are nights when I wake, half delirious, my mouth hollow and sticky with the names of other women, & have to hope that she has not heard.

There is a particular area of the sea off the East coast of China where the currents are such that they cause the air to form itself into very distinct layers so that, on occasion, light can run inside one of these layers around the curve of the earth, as though through a fibre optic cable; & so there are villages in China where, every so often, the fishermen, on going down to the ocean in the morning, will see, rising above the water, mountains & forests & lakes & small towns, that, within an hour, will disappear, resolving themselves back into an empty horizon.

Afterwards we stood by the graveside, when the grave had been filled in & covered over & all, & as I was standing there, just standing there, my brother's wife gently touched my hand, & I was riven in two by the touch of

hand touching hand skin bone hair touching

; & I turned to her, my hand held in her hand, & she took my other one &, holding them both in hers, she leant forward & softly kissed my forehead. Then she stood looking at me with her sad, grave eyes, until she gave a small, sad smile, & her hands holding my hands opened slowly, twin moons opening silently like hands touching; & for the first time since my aunt's death I began to cry.

There are nights when I wake, half delirious, and have to hope. But still, despite all this. For she will touch the five toes on my right foot, one by one, touch & hold them, as one would hold the toes or the tiny bunched fists of a baby, holds them between her thumb & forefinger, gently & firmly, & softsmilingly names them (& each time you must think: this is a chance that will not be offered you again). Except they won't become five softsmiling toes until she touches them, until she names them & owns them & allows me to own them in turn. & when she does this for me it is for this that I am. & here, at this moment, a swoopcrash of vertigo, of unrestrained headlongness –

From the graveyard we drove in silence. It grew dark quietly, quickly, stealing up around us until we wordlessly gave way. Outside, away from the glare of the halogen lamps, the night was a stumbling, rutted immersion, the ground hungry & grasping, swallowing hedges & trees & wind & clouds. & then, all of a sudden, we came upon the sea.

We must have heard it before we came upon it, but I don't remember that. I just remember cresting a hill, & all of a sudden feeling a rush of wind & salt & seaspray, & feeling in front of me a vast expanse of emptiness that tugged at my sleeves; & through the air, falling, the cries of birds (& no birds there, only their cries cutting like glass through the black transparent night air). & there were no stars there either, no stars, only the moon like a white hand opening, & white flecks on the sea luminous in the darkness, & it was as if, like in some story, the stars had fallen into the sea & had sunk down to lie, resting, on the sea-bed, & their light was being refracted up through the water, dissolved, & only now & then gleaming in the brief glint of a whitecrested wave.

There seems to be some flaw here, some flaw, maybe not in the air, but in the fabric of the air. It feels like a toy soldier that has been cast but where the two halves don't quite fit together. There is a fault-line that runs down the side.

These inconsolable jarrings of memory.

Say: In the last years my g.father turned deaf.
             When we were talking to him, we would have to write
             down our half of the conversation, & he would read what we
             had written, & answer out loud –

with words clamorous & misshapen, sentences rambling & briar-twisted, as if his mouth & brain were filling with cotton, cotton bulging & bludgeoning his brain & mouth –
(that dark-curtained room, air heavy w/ stillness & time slowly turning.)
             Kept in old notebooks, small, leather covers, old ones,
             pages turning yellowish & brittle. Writing conversations I still
             have now, somewhat cryptic & awkward, like one-sided phone
             conv.s in films.

Towards the v. end he couldn't speak, & had become too weak to write himself – so these n.books were all the conv. consisted of – an attempt at comm., launched we know not where, into the void, or some such. We know we shall never be heard.

For weeks after I knew he could no longer read I kept writing in his books. Eventually I gave up – would take them out but not have the strength to write, to face the fact that I could no longer reach him.

Last to go – touch. In the end he wouldn't even respond to that – his eyes open, no reflexes, slowly blinking.

Or say: When my g.father was dying – went blind. Would write on sheets as his vision went – as he became totally blind, would scribble over&over on the same sheet, if we left him alone, until it was tacky with ink.

Or say: When my g.father died he just passed away softly. He was lucid up to the end, but it was as if his long, measured silences just expanded until they overcame him, engulfed him; but these words are too violent – say, rather: it was as if he receded into his silences, further & further, until he passed some horizon point, & passed away, out of sight; his silences that were touched & tugged lightly by long fingers, until he was dead.

Or Declaim. Orate. Utter. Recite. Hold forth. Shout. Shriek. Yell. Cry. Howl. Wail. Roar. Kick. Bite. Bawl. Fuck. Scream.

Or say: I want to reach down the phone line & squeeze your heart until it weeps w/ overwhelming sorrow – until it weeps clear fluid that floods your chest cavity & coughs your choking lungs up raw through your bleeding throat.

– & I will promise (& not just here, in these sheerfalling moments) to always bring her roses, white in summer & red in winter, because she told me once that white roses remind her of her mother, who died in July (the memory of pain buried like splinters of glass in her soft eyes); & so she keeps only white roses in the summer, but when winter sets in, she leaves all the white roses die, & will keep only red ones until the end of the following spring. & she'll smile when I promise this, because I don't have to tell her why I'm always making these promises, because she already knows & because she loves me regardless.

There's a piece of music by a Jewish composer, Artur Amichai, called *Mechanical Piece for Unfinished Piano*. It was completed some time in February 1938 & first performed at a private function in Prague in March of that year, eight months before Amichai would die of tuberculosis. It's an unusual piece for a few reasons – there's no extant recording of it, & no surviving copy of the score. The only record we have of it is a description of its first, &, presumably, its only, performance, in Volume Two of the eighteen-volume first edition of *Die Musik in Geschichte und Gegenwart*, where there is a brief biography of Amichai that is omitted from all subsequent editions. The biography is written by a Bernd Sponheuer, who was present at that performance of Amichai's piece, & describes it as series of eight movements in sonata form, a series of eight inverted variations that builds throughout to its unstated theme. These variations are scored for a piano in various stages of completion – the first movement is played using only the inner metal frame of the piano (which, we are told, must be strong enough to support the enormous tension the strings impose – approximately 18 tons), the second movement is played on the metal frame & the soundboard, & so on; the fifth movement is played on the frame, soundboard, bridges, action & outer wooden case, the seventh on the entire piano less the keys & pedals, & the eighth on the entire piano less only the keys. In order to accomplish this, the performance took place in eight different rooms, each featuring a piano in the requisite state of construction, while the audience were moved from one room to another between each pair of movements. Unfortunately, Sponheuer does not record for precisely what parts of the piano the third, fourth or sixth movements are scored, & so we have no idea, apart from our own guesswork, how these particular movements would have sounded. He describes *Mechanical Piece for Unfinished Piano* as a series of variations "ending, inevitably, before its theme can be fully realised, before the music can reach a conclusion in its full expression."

Driving back I sat in the backseat & looked through the window at miles & miles of forest going past. Dusk settled like ashes on the leaves. & I remember it felt like we were driving into the mouth of the night, into this great yawning maw, & right down through its labyrinthine gut into its stomach & liver & spleen; & beyond the trees, on either side, huge rolling mountains, enormous & distant & dark, & it felt as if, between them, we were trapped in the gravity of their immense bulk, & could only drift uncertainly onwards; & as the light seeped slowly out, I could no longer see them, only, beyond the faint, greyfeathered shadows of the trees, a more enormous dark; yet I could still feel their pull & hear the whisper of their gravity crackle like static running over my skin, lost in the darkness, like the sea at night.

Joelle Pedersen

Flowers for Charlie

In April of 1955, three days before his thirteenth birthday, my brother Charlie got Polio. We had just moved to Lowville in upstate New York. I was nine. It had finally warmed up outside, and there was Queen Anne's Lace everywhere. Queen Anne's Lace usually grows in the late summer, and I have always wondered why the flowers bloomed so early that year. Don't pick them, my sister Meg had told me. It will make the Virgin Mary sad. They're her favorite. I took her warning very seriously. I would stay in the middle of the road on the way home from school so as not to crush the flowers as I walked. One day, I was weeding our garden and pulled some out by mistake. I ran over to Meg, crying. She laughed. You've done it now, Aggy, she said. When Charlie got sick, I was sure it was my fault.

It happened very fast. Charlie had always been healthy, except for a headache which bothered him sometimes. One day he came home saying that he was sore, but my father told him it must have been from gym class. Charlie went to bed early. When he asked to stay home from school the next morning, my father didn't let him. He was a pastor. Do you think Jesus took sick days, he asked Charlie. Do you think John the Baptist or Saint Paul ever stayed in bed?

No, sir, Charlie said, and that was it. He put on his red hi-top sneakers and went to school. When we were eating dinner that night, Charlie fell asleep at the table. His face landed in a plate of mashed butternut squash. My little brother Ralph laughed, and my father glared. Meg's eyes got very big – she was the oldest. Charlie was put to bed. Dr. Peterson came and shut the door to Charlie's room. I looked through the hole we had made in the wall between our bedrooms, and saw the doctor wrapping Charlie all over in white gauze. It looked like he'd broken every bone in his body. The air smelled like wet wool.

I could tell my mother was very upset. She pretended that nothing had happened, but she began boiling all our water, and washing each dish two or three times. She cleaned the toilet every day. She made us get rid of Suzie, our old Bassett hound. She said we couldn't eat meat anymore. She only wore her good apron, and her face was getting yellow. I don't understand it, she would tell the ladies who came to our house with Rhubarb pie and oatmeal cookies (I always hoped for chocolate-chip). Charlie was a good boy. He never played in the dirt or the cold; he was too busy doing his schoolwork. And I keep them so clean, she would always add. The women would nod, as if they understood, but they just looked glad they weren't her.

Charlie had to stay in bed. I couldn't see him, except through the hole in the wall. I would talk to him sometimes, about how I wanted him to get better, and how I missed Suzie, but he never answered me. One day I tried to slip him some jellybeans under the door. My mother saw, and pulled me down the stairs so hard that my elbow hurt. Go sit on the couch until dinnertime, she told me. Every day the doctor came, and every day my father would read the Bible to Charlie. No one else went into Charlie's room.

We didn't celebrate Charlie's birthday that year. There was no cake, or presents, and no one said anything about it. We didn't really celebrate Easter either. Usually we would have the whole family over: my cousins and grandfather and everyone. It was my mother's favorite holiday – she would make Cornish hens and cut up little pieces of green apple into star shapes for the salad. We'd melt chocolate and make pops shaped like baby chicks for our baskets, and sometimes even have an egg hunt. But the Easter when Charlie was sick, no one came. Me, Meg and Ralph went with my father to church. We came back and had some cold ham and mashed potatoes with the skins still in that my mother had prepared, even though she knew I never ate the skins. My father said a long grace, and asked us about Jesus in the Garden to see if we had been paying attention during church. That was Easter.

Then things got much worse. Charlie had to go away, my mother said. To a hospital in the city, where they could take better care of him. Meg got very angry at this. It's not fair, she said. I want to go to the city, away from here. Later, a big black car came to our house for Charlie. It was long so that he could lie down all the way in the back. We watched through the kitchen window.

That's a hearse, Meg told me, in the tone she always used when she wanted people to remember that she was fifteen. It belongs to daddy's friend Mr. Bruce, the undertaker. It's a car for dead people.

But Charlie's not dead, I said, confused.

Not yet he's not, she said.

Charlie didn't come home for a long time. My father would take our car to visit Charlie every weekend, leaving Friday afternoon and coming back on Sunday morning. Usually he would be tired for church, or late. A few times he missed the morning service. He began to talk too much about Job and would rest his eyes when the choir was singing. One Sunday when he was preaching, his glasses fell off his face and landed in a cup of water. Ralph laughed. Each week fewer people were at church, and after a while they started to complain. The old ladies didn't try to talk to me and Meg and Ralph anymore, which was alright because I had never known what to say to them. I would sometimes hear the ladies talking about my mother at coffee hour. I didn't say anything, because my father had told me to respect my elders and to be seen but not heard and things. I wanted to though. After a while, we had the first row of pews at church to ourselves, which I thought was strange because everyone always wants to sit in the front. Once I woke up in the middle of the night to get a glass of water from the kitchen and saw my father sitting on our couch in the dark. I ran back to bed before he saw me.

June came, and Charlie was still not back. That summer was the longest one I can remember. We had to stay inside. The adults were always talking in low voices, eating butterscotch cookies and drinking black tea. They didn't want us to know, but I have very good hearing. It wasn't just Charlie. The Polio was spreading in Lowville. This is what Mrs. Herbert had been saying to Mrs. Murphy after church one Sunday afternoon. Suddenly, there were no more bike races for anyone, no trips to summer houses. The red bathing suit my mother had just bought me was put in the attic – the town pool was closed, she told me, and so I had no use for it. The ice cream truck would drive down the street, playing music over and over, but no one would come out. Eventually there was no more ice cream truck either. Then the summer baseball league was canceled. On that Fourth of July, Lowville did not have fireworks. They weren't even selling hot dogs at the supermarket down the street. We don't want the meat to be undercooked, my mother explained to me when I asked her why we couldn't have a barbeque. I nodded silently, but really I was angry. I love barbeques, and I didn't think it was fair that we weren't having one just because of everybody with Polio. I was still fine, after all.

As the Queen Anne's Lace grew higher along the side of the road, I became more and more convinced that I had made Charlie get sick, and more and more convinced that I had to do something to bring him back. Every night, I prayed to the Virgin Mary, and told her how sorry I was for picking her favorite flower. I would pray in all different positions – lying down in my bed, on my knees, with my eyes closed, and folding my hands like my father had showed me. I would pray for a very long time. But the Virgin Mary didn't hear. Meg gave me her rabbit's foot and a penny which she said was lucky to put in the collection plate at church, but the usher taking the offering just smiled at me with tight lips and gave them back. I tried taking some seeds from our shed out back and planting new flowers. They were pansy seeds, and pansies are very pretty flowers, so I was sure the Virgin Mary would like them. But the flowers grew, and wilted, and Charlie was not home.

So I started to make a fort for Charlie. He had always talked about how much he wanted a fort, and I thought that if he had one, he might decide to come home. I worked on it every day. I would tell my mother that I was going next door to Jenny Bergman's, because I always went to Jenny's. She didn't know that Jenny's parents had told her a long time ago not to have me over. Sneaking down the street and into the woods was easy since there was no one outside to see. I would follow the path of Queen Anne's Lace into the field, past the trees, careful never to step on the flowers. In the swampy heat, I would clear brush and pull pieces of wood from the old, rotting fence that ran through the field.

Charlie really liked old western movies, and so I built the fort like a tepee. I made the boards cross at the very top, and tied them together with long grass and weeds. I left an opening at the front where we could crawl in. I covered the ground outside the fort with pine needles so it would be soft. I even tried to make a fireplace, but I couldn't remember exactly how they did it in the movies. It was hard work, and I worked on it for weeks. Some days I pretended I was a young squaw named Pretty-Flower, and that I was building the tepee to protect my brother from the evil white men. Other days I wondered what they were doing to Charlie in the hospital. I had heard of people who had Polio being put on machines that breathed for them, and I hoped very much that this wasn't what was happening. Once in a while, I thought about how Charlie used to make me sneak downstairs with him late at night to watch the Indians fighting the cowboys on TV. The picture was always fuzzy, and Charlie would keep the sound on mute so no one could hear us. One night I had knocked a heavy book off the coffee table. We had thought for sure it would wake our parents.

Shhhhh, Aggy, Charlie had whispered to me. If Mom and Dad come down, you gotta crawl under the couch, ok? That way they won't see you.

But there's only enough room for one of us underneath the couch, I had whispered back. What are you gonna do?

He had looked at me very seriously. You know how on TV,

sometimes the chief has to die so the rest of the Indians don't get killed?

I had nodded.

It's like that, he had said.

Remembering this made me sad though, and usually I just tried to think about building the fort so Charlie would come home. But even when I finished the fort, Charlie was not back.

I didn't see my brother again until the very end of the summer. We were getting ready to go back to school – it was the last week of August. The air was dead, heavy with the kind of heat that makes you feel like the world has stopped moving. I knew he was coming home before anyone told me, because my mother made chocolate-chip waffles for breakfast. They were Charlie's favorite, and we hadn't had them since he left.

After breakfast, my mother sat us down in the parlor, which we could never usually go in. Your brother is better, she said. He's coming home. The sun shone through the blinds and the light made a striped pattern all over my mother and the rest of the room. Ralph bit into his sucker.

Meg looked confused. But I thought he was supposed to die, she said. I looked away, but I was smiling on the inside.

That afternoon my mother sat us down again. Before your brother can come back, we all need to get a shot, she said. The doctor will be here very soon, and I want you on your best behavior. Understand? We all nodded because you don't disagree with my mother. But Meg's face looked stiff, and probably mine did too. I hate the doctor more than anything. I thought about the time when I had been playing barefoot down the street and had stepped on a piece of glass. My father had carried me inside and put me to bed. When Doctor Peterson came, he had given me some medicine that had made me feel very sleepy. Then he had told me that I couldn't play outside for a long time and always should wear shoes. I hate wearing shoes a lot.

My mother made us sit in the parlor without talking until the doctor finally came. I was very surprised, because I had thought it would be Dr. Peterson. This doctor was new, very blonde and very tall. I could tell he was young. His face reminded me of Suzie. He was wearing a dark grey suit, which I thought was silly because in Lowville the only time you ever wore a suit was at church. The man said his name was Dr. Puskar, and then I remembered hearing about him. Mrs. Philips had said to Mrs. Amato that he was a specialist from New York City, and that he knew how to cure the Polio. My mother shook his hand and tightened her bun. They both looked very nervous. We all watched as Dr. Puskar sat down and opened his black bag. I wanted to play with the gauze, but I knew my mother wouldn't allow it. The doctor pulled out a large needle and took the cap off of it. My heart began to beat fast and I tried to swallow but my throat was too tight. The needle was longer than my hand, and very thick. Ralph began to cry.

No way, Meg said. Charlie can stay in the hospital for the rest of his life. You're not putting that in my arm.

My mother glared.

Dr. Puskar smiled with half his face. It will be okay little one, he said quietly. He picked up the needle with a shaky hand and continued looking through the bag. We were all very still. Suddenly, he stood up and turned to my mother. Ah, well, Mrs. Hubbard, I do apologize, but it appears I have left the vaccine at my office. I'm afraid I'm going to have to go back and get it quickly. He had an accent which I didn't recognise, and slurred his words like a record player does when it's on the slowest speed.

My mother nodded very slightly, but the wrinkles in her forehead showed. You're sure this is going to work, she asked him.

I'm afraid I don't know, M'am, Dr. Puskar said. Then he turned and left without looking at any of us. The needle was still sitting on our kitchen table.

No one moved. I stared at the needle. I felt my shoulders tense, and a sharp pain in the middle of my stomach. It was suddenly very cold. The air pressed against my skin. This made me remember my old goldfish Henry and how he had looked when Ralph took him out of the bowl, how his mouth had pinched together and how he had flapped his fins as he lay on the cement in front of our house, and then my mother put him in the freezer. I had cried a lot. We buried Henry in the backyard, next to the vegetable garden. I had put him in a little heart-shaped box, and my father made me say the blessing. We never got another fish.

I sat at the table for a very long time. I began to feel so sick that I had to put my head down. I closed my eyes and thought about Charlie, and how much I wanted him to come home. My mother walked up from behind and shook me. Agnes, wake up, she said. The doctor will be back soon.

I still have a little scar on my left arm from the shot, but I didn't even cry when I got it.

The next day, Charlie came home in the same black car. He was very weak, Meg told me, and my father had to carry him upstairs straight to bed even though he was thirteen. I looked through the peephole and saw him asleep. When he woke up, my mother told us it would be alright to go talk to him. I ran outside right away, because I wanted to bring Charlie flowers. But the August heat had killed everything in my mother's garden, and the only flowers that had survived were the Queen Anne's Lace. It still grew wild everywhere. I quickly picked a bouquet and ran upstairs, into Charlie's room, not even stopping to knock.

I looked at my brother very closely. He was white, as if he hadn't ever been out in the sun. His face wasn't as round as it used to be, and his skin looked tight like someone had pulled it back. He sat far down in his sheets, but his breathing was very loud. There was a wheelchair in the corner of the room. I placed the flowers on the nightstand.

Hi Charlie, I said.

Hi Aggy, he said.

There was a long silence. I didn't know what else to say.

It's been really hot here, I said to him eventually, speaking very fast. And I built a fort. It's not really very big, but I think maybe it could fit two people. I made it just like those teepees on TV. It has a door and a fireplace and everything. We can go see it right now if you want.

Charlie smiled and laughed quietly. You know Aggy, I'm really still kind of tired, so I think I should sleep. We can go some other time though. Alright?

I looked at him, nodding. Alright, I said. I turned to leave. Charlie, are you going to be okay? I asked him.

He shifted in his bed. Yeah, I will, he said. I think I'll be okay.

Okay, I said. I thought about things for a moment. Charlie, what was it like? To have Polio, I asked.

He closed his eyes slowly. I thought he was going to sleep. The hospital was awful, he said. I didn't want to be there. But when I was on the breathing machine, sometimes I would have dreams that I was flying. Those were nice.

I didn't really understand, but I smiled anyways. I brought you some flowers, I said. Momma says they're weeds, but I think they're kind of pretty.

I know, he said. Thanks, Aggy. I like them too.

Maria Lisogorskaya

Matthew Drage

Meat and Medicine

One night, shortly after our arrival, we went to a small bar in the east of the yellow-walled city. Our palms sweated with the card games. We stooped through a stairwell to find the beginnings of another orgy.

The final game was tense. A fat Mafioso was beside us, eating old chewing tobacco, and coughing into our faces. He sat back in his chair, and looked, piggy-eyed, at my friend. John blushed.

We accepted our winnings with dignity. Girls helped it all along. The piggy-eyed man had taken off his clothes, and his flesh enveloped John. I sat in anticipation. The dark grimy room, and the stool over which John was pushed, creaked. We swapped, and things were reversed. We all came. The man beat us soundly.

Weighted fists knocked us out of the back door. In the street, outside the shops and restaurants, men played cards in groups. That night, many people were dressed up and clumped around fires eating roasted meat. Crowds fucked in the alleys in screaming droves. John and I followed a loud group around, wishing we could speak the language. We marched with everyone into the centre of the city, and watched the girls and boys dance around something like a maypole in the middle of the square.

When the dance had finished, they took their clothes off. Some of the audience joined them, and some carried on eating. We crouched in a corner. Listening to the sounds of the orgy, our interest grew. Later that night, we trawled through the wiry grass, and back to our flat. We slept there in the same bed. We rested unevenly, our hearts pushing leftover poison around our bodies like water being swept. The excess spilt over as sweat and piss. His legs were longer than mine, and I spent some time looking at his feet sticking out from under the covers.

Dr. Stevens, the only doctor in the city who spoke our language, came round the next day. He gestured for us to lay us down again on our bed, shot us up, and we slept. We awoke with our left arms bandaged. Two round and sweaty technicians cleared up around us, slotting and clicking syringes into steel cases. The doctor kissed us both good-bye, and the three of them left. I stood up. John, his movements and speech slow and happy from the medicine, suggested that we take a drive around the city. He walked out in front of me, and kicked dirt up in bright little clouds that I waded through as I followed him.

It was dark by the time we approached the train station. I'd had to drive slowly through the cafes, which spread themselves out across the streets. As we passed the whores and the tramps who drunk meths, I saw the doctor again. He went into a pharmacy. The place was shiny; it cut a clean square into the crumbled walls. It was very full, and the light in its window projected a hard green glow into the faces of those under its glare. John and I pulled up, and, faces close, we watched the doctor as he queued. The doctor looked back, saw us, and nodded. John sat back in his seat, and stretched, his back arched, his left shoulder rubbing up against the hot plastic of the car door.

I waited until the doctor had left the pharmacy, and then softly opened the car door. John shut it behind me, and started playing with the radio. Scuffing his soft leather shoes, Dr. Stevens walked away in small, sharp steps, a brown parcel under his arm. I stayed about twenty feet behind him.

He stopped at the edge of the road, and waited to cross. I caught up with him and tapped him on the shoulder. He did not start - rather, he swallowed quickly and deliberately, and glanced up and then down the street. He took my hand, led me to the station toilets, and I reached down his trousers. He did not look at me once until he had come.

Smile locked, he handed me a small white package. He opened the door, and, white light on his back, shuddered out into the dark.

John and I took a trip out to the moist, oily industrial sector to meet our friend Mr. Smith. Mr. Smith had been living in the city for fifteen years. With short plods he limped towards us, eyes unfocused, and leaned into my open window. He had a high hairline and a grey-red face. His arms and hands hung down, smooth and puffy, and cheeks his were round and well-marbled. Over each side of the window his neck hung, in tight little flaps. "What are you two doing down here?" he asked.

"We were wondering if you needed any help." I answered.

"I need some new boots." He said. He stepped back a few paces to show us. He laughed, but his breath wasn't in it. John smiled politely.

"Where are we going tonight?" he asked Mr. Smith.

"Down to the tracks. There's plenty of junk lying round at the moment. I only need to fill one more order, and it might be enough. I'm close to getting out of here."

We picked up a few things from the sides of the tracks - two railway sleepers, a roll of wire, some short lengths of scaffold. There were also some computers. Their insides spilt out onto the gravel. Everything went in neat rows in the back of his rusting and peeling truck, lined up, tied down with rope, and braced with corrugated cardboard. Back in the tidy, oily, high-ceilinged warehouse, we laid everything down in a line. The rafters were rusty and black with soot. Long white strip lights hung off them, swinging slightly in the wind that blew through the glassless windows. There was bird shit, but no birds.

Mr. Smith set upon the computers, pulling them slowly apart with pliers and a screwdriver. He had old typesetting drawers set in another line across the back of the warehouse, into which he filed the pieces. Piled up against the left wall were dozens of crates, packed up and ready for collection. As quietly as I could, I walked up behind him, and looked over his sweaty shoulders. I watched him as he twisted out transistors with desperate care, using his short white fingers. John picked up a shard of glass from the floor, and dragged it across his wrist. He grinned again at both of us as we sat cross-legged next to the typesetters' drawers. We grinned back, and watched the blood drip.

I picked out a small test tube from a rack at my left hand, and threw it over to Mr. Smith. He didn't catch it, and it broke and chimed. I threw another, which he didn't miss. Mr. Smith sucked up some blood with a pipette, squirted it onto the test tube, and put it into the fridge. Flooding in and out of my head and ears was the sound of all of our hearts beating. I scooped some blood up with my fingers. It was mixed with the oily dirt from the floor.

I took John's hand, and rubbed his bloody wrist into my palm. My hand felt like wrought iron. We kissed and held our hands together in silence, listening to the drips. His face felt cold and clammy against mine.

We went back to the flat again just before dawn, dried out and red from walking and sweating. Although the lights were working, I could not see very well, and I tripped over the concrete step up to the shower. John spent the night staring out of the window, picking skin off his hands.

Later that morning, I told John that I needed to go and find Dr Stevens at the train station. "We should go into town to buy some meat first," John replied. "I planned to meet a girl at the market. You'll like her."

At ten-to-four down in the market, we met Mary. John talked

too much. We moved down the slope of the marketplace, the three of us, passing through the smell of meat and plastic. We saw a tiny fruit stall. It sold only rotting figs, and a single one cost a month's food vouchers. "I didn't know there was any more fruit to sell," said Mary, almost interested. We walked in silence for a few dozen steps. Mary spoke again.

"By the way, I hear old Mr. Smith was killed last night. Shot in the face by the border guards."

"Was he indeed?" John asked. The words almost caught as he spoke. I looked at my feet, and came up smiling. John looked at me for a while, and I started to laugh. I laughed too loud and high for too long.

"I understand," said John to Mary as we began the walk home, "that you've been feeling off-colour. We'll call our doctor later, and I'm sure he'll be a great help. He's always very generous."

"What do you mean?"

"A pint of blood and some hair should do it," replied John.

"You know, I think he's ill now too," I said.

"Yes. We might outlast him," said John.

Back in the flat, we prepared lunch. I cut up the very last of the onions, slicing them half way down the centre, then removing the skin, and dicing them so that they fell in small cubes on the board. We all sat down and watched them fry. There were very few people with any cooking equipment at all, any more. We had little gas, but sometimes we cooked for the smell. Ignoring the instructions on the packet, we'd once fried onions with some factory meat. The meat was made to be eaten raw. Neither of us slept for days afterwards, and John gave up vomiting in the toilet, which had stopped flushing.

"Let's get going. I have to visit my family," I said, as I tipped the onions out of the window.

"Alright," said John. "We'll drop you off, then see if we can find a way into the warehouse. The police won't have moved everything out yet. There might still be something for us to take."

"I'll drop you two off. I don't like you using the car," I replied.

I dropped John and Mary off at the warehouse, and made my way up to the house. It was on a steep hill. The road up to it wound yellow and red out of the industrial sector, and dribbled out into the hills for a way, until it hit a neat fence. That fence was strung taut around the whole town, and was lined with patrols.

I took the car up the hill fast. I wanted to hit someone on the way. I had heard that they sometimes moved prisoners around the country. Left to rot, we were worse off than prisoners.

Using the key that I'd had cut, I unlocked the front door. The hall was squat, and the stairs overhung and made me want to duck as I stepped inside. The carpets were brown and grey, and they stuck out at me against the dusty yellows of the southern light. Mother sat bunched-up in the corner of the living room, and called over to me. "There's... a jug of tea. In the fridge. Please, do have some." She spat a little as she spoke.

"Yes Mother."

"I hope things are well with you. Your job... is going well I trust. You look very well." She stared at the wall with a smile, and was silent. I got some tea from the fridge. Mother wouldn't let anyone boil the kettle. She brewed tea for days, lukewarm on the windowsill. I brought it back in with me, and we sat, Mother and I, in the pastel living room, which was very much like the hallway. We did not discuss anything. Then my sister came downstairs. She complained sourly about a man having made a rude gesture to her in the street. Through her nose, she demanded of me why he should have done it, and what could possibly have moved him. She continued in this way for some time, all the while moving her hands around each other in a fast rubbing motion.

"Mother?" I said, interrupting my sister. Both she and my mother flinched. "I am going to take some meat from the fridge. It seems that you have an awful lot." My sister glared at me for a while. I sipped my tea from its plastic teacup. Her legs began to move in small jerks, and her glare became glassy. Her shoeless feet hit the floor in a jagged patter. I thought she might have been fitting, but I didn't wait to see. I would ask the doctor to check up on her. I shoved all their meat into a carrier bag, along with three bottles of purified water.

A man shouted at me in French or Italian or whatever the language there was, as I rolled down the street, clutch down and windows open. I wondered how my sister's fit was progressing, and smiled, and sung to myself.

I returned to the warehouse to find that a single policeman was guarding the front door. I asked the officer what was happening. He replied, and, when he saw that I could not understand him, he spat on my left foot. It dried quickly in the afternoon sun.

If followed a little further, the road would take me to the back of the warehouse. Gravel loose on the hot dusty concrete under my feet, I rounded the corner and walked up to the back door. I pushed it open. It scraped because it was rusty, but not loudly. I went inside, catching my arms against the edges of the corrugated iron. I couldn't see to start with. Things looked blue and dark. I unfolded myself, and looked around with new eyes. The stacked palettes had gone, and the typesetters' drawers were empty. I made my way to the toilets, and smelt blood as I opened the door.

Mary and John had not done each other so much harm. They emerged from a cubicle, and untangled themselves from each other's torn flesh. They put on their clothes, which quickly went patchy and red. I drove them to Dr. Stevens. On the back seat they lay, stinging and calm together.

John said, from behind Mary's ear, "I intended to go further, you know."

"Well," I replied, "it's for the best that you didn't. I need you both around for a while." That night, I beat John until his blood covered my hands.

Without John, I drove to the train station again in the morning. He had gone out with Mary to get more meat and medicine. I saw the doctor doing his rounds on the platform, so I got out and sat on a low brick wall. The platform was always scattered with people with nowhere to live. It was covered, and it was still heated because someone had forgotten to cut the power. People slid around slow and ill, or sat, spread out on cardboard or ragged sheets. Dr. Stevens drifted between groups like a bee moving between stinking flowers. His grin was shut up tight. For no reason at all, it seemed, he gave away his small white packages to those greeny-grey huddles of people.

He walked towards me with his short, sharp steps. "Good evening Doctor," I said to him.

"How are you feeling today? Have you come to settle the books?" he asked, smiling with pale teeth all the while.

"Not just yet. I'm going to send a girl along later for you." I had a thought. "You know, my sister needs seeing to pretty soon. You could pay her a visit tomorrow. Take whatever you find there. They won't stop you. Here's the address. That will more than cover it." I wrote out my family's address in block-capitals on the back of the receipt from the market, and handed it to him. He read it, then read the receipt. His smile did not change.

"I'm glad you're eating well," he said, with an earnest look. He laughed, and coughed. There was a little blood on his lips.

I drove back through the city, up the streets that wound in coils to the market square, and then out into the industrial estate. The factories lay brown and fallow. I was pleased that my debts had been settled at so low a price, and decided to celebrate. I went to find John and Mary, who had been sitting watching the cars under a dead olive tree, which twisted up from the dust between two blocks of flats. They were cross-legged and smoking spindly rollups. The sun glowed, orange and comforting against their faces through the smoke. I joined them. They sat close, their arms touching. I leant back, letting my head sit on the ground and bringing my knees up. We would, I told them, be getting all the medical care we needed for a while. I pulled an olive twig apart between my fingers.

"I'm not sure I'd want him in my house," said John.

"Why not?" I spoke louder than I had intended.

"He would take more than one might wish."

"He'll only take what he needs."

"That's what I meant," he said. I felt sick, and for this I almost resolved to hurt him badly. But then John slid himself over, and slowly leant back, resting his head next to mine in the dust. I forgot all about the matter. The three of us warmed together in the shade of the olive tree, and I fell asleep.

I watched the couple through closed eyes. Their mouths moved in machined synchrony. Air was forced out of from one onto the face of the other. I could see it in noisy clouds. I watched them and gave them sound. They were discussing the ground. John told Mary that he had, the previous day, drunk a mixture of the city's dirt and the blood of a girl he had once known (which he had kept in his freezer, behind the peas). It had cleared his head wonderfully. Mary laughed graciously. She laughed more as he told her something too quiet for me to hear. I shut my eyes and sound scraped in, clashing with my thoughts.

"So what did you do?" Mary asked of John.

"I phoned strangers up until I fell asleep." She looked at him, then kissed him. I opened my eyes, and sat up. I could not see very well, but it looked as if the two were still kissing. My sight cleared slightly, and I saw that John was grabbing handfuls of the ground with his free hand. I pushed my own fingers into the dirt. It was still warm from the day. The engines of the cars that passed chuckled at me.

I walked as fast as I could around the corner of a building. A dog and a child watched me vomit from the other side of the street. A man with a beard and too few clothes pushed them along.

Around the block, around the whores bowed over in hooks to snag passers-by, I continued. I was soon at the station. I slid down against a wall, unable to stand any longer. I shivered, and closed my eyes. Some time later, Dr Stevens joined me. He pushed right up next to me, and I shook softly against him. He offered me something special.

I awoke somewhere different, dead grass between my fingers. I felt a warmish sting on the back of my neck. I was grinning. I reached up and felt blood and glass. I looked at my wrist. It too was bleeding.

There was a long cut from the base of my thumb to my elbow. There was a used syringe to my right.

My lips felt like they would tear, I was grinning so hard. I walked hard back towards where I thought the olive tree might have been, stamping down into the floor, which I could not see any more.

I rounded another corner, and the street began to blacken.

Cold between John and Mary, I looked at the morning with grey eyes. I ached, and my mouth was sour. My forearm was green and blue. I stood up, and looked down at my friend and his lover. The sheets were bloody, and they were dead. I put what was useful in the freezer, and left.

Richard Freeman

stupid, prying goose

October 25th.
5.46 pm. Outside. Brighton is warm and wet.

Someone is making a film that might never be shown, more of a
labour of love. The film will be post-modern and fractured; identical
to the efforts of his documentary filmmaking classmates. The night
course is up soon, and this aspiring director knows that his supervisor
will hate this submission. He doesn't care. It's coming from the heart.
Narrative in this muggy Brighton month is disjointed and unfriendly,
the director is positioning himself and walking around, trying, but fail-
ing, to capture a world he is yet to figure out. There are two other
cameras in the city, trying to achieve the same, trying to make sense of
something. This director sits on a bus, hoping that the people around
him will write themselves a story. He will see how the others have
done later. At the front of the Brighton & Hove double-decker, the
autumn afternoon is sweaty and dulled. Three stony-faced suits, two
anoraks and one perambulator rest at the front of the lower deck.
Pairs of eyes all along the bus flick and glance across at a little old
woman snarling at everyone else, or herself – it isn't clear. Her tatty
bags clumped next to her take up the bulk of the double-seat as she
seems to curse the world under her breath. She must be nearly ninety,
the driver thinks. Should be in a bloody home. The old lady, actually
seventy-nine, is thinking about the rainy city, her cat, Michael Moore,
Jesus, and what life was like when she could see properly. She would
have taken the car, but she only wanted to get groceries from town.
Seems silly to drive in weather like this. She clutches her basket of
apples as the brand new bus trundles through the drizzle.
        Her prolonged cold is making her sniff and gurgle involuntari-
ly, she will giggle about it later; 'it's quite embarrassing' she envisages
telling her daughter over a glass of Rioja. But now, here: the little
woman is unaware that the bus of sour-faces are collectively, silently,
in unknowing conspiracy, looking at her with unfriendly eyeballs.
There was definitely more than one person sitting on that bus think-

ing of the old lady as a haggard old witch. Probably come into Brighton to steal a pigeon for a pie; maybe even a child, thinks a bespectacled gentleman two rows back and to the right. At the back of the bus, a teenage couple smirk at the thought of getting old and vocally accuse each other of smelling like piss. The old lady is blissful, as if in spite. She had always been confident and self-assured, but couldn't go on denying the arthritis and creeping cataracts for much longer. Forty-seven years as an actress and singer gives you all the self-assurance you need, her daughters would constantly assure her (a little narrative joke; she smirks at her reflection in the window). The bus jolts to a halt as the BUS STOPPING sign lights up.

Brighton Old Steine jitters and flickers outside of the window. Ruth wonders how old it could really be. She watches imaginary Dinosaurs basking in the central fountain under thunderous prehistoric palm-trees. She remembers that she's old, glares at the bus driver as she helps herself onto the pavement, basket under her arm, her eyes catch the sunshine reflected on the concrete. She loves the birds and the huddles of foreign students getting splashed and lost. A huge grin starts to spread across her face. What a funny old day, she thinks as she waddles and jerks across the traffic islands. A cake day. She grins even wider: sponge, icing and chocolate for the children. An apple crumble for the others, maybe filled with razors. She looks down at the grocer's apples in her basket. I want it to be sweet, sickly and naughty. I'll show them that Grandma's good for something. A seagull starts to walk towards her, but thinks better of it and flies upwards and south towards the sea.

Brighton has been Ruth Margaret Millicent McCabe's home for the last seven years (Ruth is the old woman, she's now happy to reveal that). She couldn't deny that her old country home had become too much. Too much since Jim kicked the bucket, popped his plimsolls, no…that's not funny yet. Death is still something subversive to Ruth, it would have been easier if Jim had just run away. At the time, her eldest daughter (Bronwyn…no…yes, OK you can know that too) offered her a place to stay with her and the two children. Ruth would never admit it to anyone else, but the move was one of the best things she had ever done. But it wasn't easy, she hated looking like a charity case. She wanted to put off looking like a charity case until she was one. Ruth edges her way towards bustling St. James' Street, taking her time when crossing the roads. Slow, waddle…that's it. The sun seems to beat down stronger and stickier; she can feel it heating it up her nape. Bzzuz bzzuz sigh the Supermarket doors, but Ruth was already jostling towards the first aisle. It was time to make those children smile. God knows they need it…. a smile. Or a clip 'round the ear. There was shopping to do.

The cameraman's gaze agrees. Bzzuz. Bzzuz.

5.46 pm Kemptown Village. The teatime grimace.

'I done the chicken first.' A second camera is filming this conversation. 'I'm going to do aisle four now. Tell Andy that I'll take over at six,' mumbles Alex. And fuck off while you're doing it. You fat cunt. She balances a tin of peas under her chin and puts another two on the shelf at eye-level. Why does she have to watch me all the time? It's not as if… God, she's a fucking moron. Alexandra Ella Mansfield picks up the printed list from the floor. Trying to wipe off a footprint, she ends up smudging the top three lines; in her eyes there is a determination to get this done soon. 'What does that say, Tim?' She suddenly realises that she can see down this man's throat. Too, too close, mister.

'Chicken? I done the chicken first. I'll keep on doing the meat.'

'Tim, chicken ain't meat.'

'Whatever.' Tim really doesn't seem to care. She can still smell his stale gum breath as she turns away. She makes her way quickly over to the chilled meats. Catching her reflection in a metal display rack, she pauses. She imagines herself naked, rubbing herself up against the bakery display. The camera keeps back, so as not to be seen in shot. I think the cameraman has an erection. The heady smell of the packaged animals doesn't affect this supershopworker anymore; to Alex the air smells more like the incense at her local church: desperate and dying. It would always amaze Alex that working in a Supermarket with twenty-four other people at any given time, with aisles full of fat drunks and blind shoppers, that you could still feel completely alone; no bastards to smile at. £3.10 for sixty minutes of her life. As a joke, later this evening, she envisages telling her friends that she would feel less cheap if she was a Kemptown whore. It's unlikely that they will disagree, leaving the joke hanging awkwardly.

She still has four aisles to clear, it is her mission to finish early. She will see if the faithful Cara is about this evening. They could get a bottle of cider and watch a video at home. Alex stops. She thinks her tatty apron pocket is vibrating. Still. No. Nothing. She takes out her chipped mobile telephone to check for missed calls. Back to the cold meats.

'Why me?' Alex stares up at two swollen faces above her; each greased with butter and juvenile insecurity. One minute passes, breaking the flow (this would all be edited to an appropriate soundtrack later.)

'But why did Cocksure say that I had to clean it up?' The smug faces trail off now that they have answered her question, proudly leaving Alex with a mop, bucket and a raised middle finger. She finds the spillage of Cranberry Splash two aisles left, and gets on to her knees to start scrubbing. Cunts, cunts, cunts, cunts, cunts, cunts. The suddy puddle on the floor looks like she has wretched up bile, she can just about see the ugly, twisted profiles of the Jones sisters dancing in it. They were thankless and spoilt, milking every wink from Cocksure, every dribble of praise that they received from Head Office. She reckoned they were being boned by the lot of them. Double-incest, anal favours. She spat in the water. They had absolutely no right to even be alive, but she knew that there was no point in arguing. Alex cleans the mess up as quickly as possible; the thrill of resuming aisle duties is all consuming. As she returns the cleaning materials to the information desk, she darts past the piles and piles of cheap, farce-trade fruits and vegetables, Halloween pumpkins on display like fat heads. They all smell rotten to her, as if existing in a shop like this would decrease anyone's self-life. They die as soon as they arrive Looking at the time, she shrieks; she is supposed to take over from Andy at six. She's not working quickly enough. At times like this she needs a magic wand to stop time. The camera operator presses pause, and is not quite sure what to make of this woman. A mind like ice. He considers masturbating, but decides to wait.

5.46 pm Madeira Drive. Ten minutes from Kemptown shopping village.

Carter Prince Laine moved to East Sussex from California seventeen years ago. *He bends down, back straight, brushes a fleck of tar from his moccasins.* Seventeen long years ago, but it was all swell. The third camera watches this man from across the street, tracking every movement, interpreting an inner-monologue. Carter has made enough money and respect to write a worthy autobiography. And to cap it all, gee!, his Mother was visiting this weekend. *What he thinks is dandruff turns out to be sea salt.* Carter thinks to himself about his own precision. Keep one eye on the road in front, one on the mirror and one on the people riding with you. Swell advice. *Carter's eyes hurt. It works only in theory.* Crossing the road to avoid a sitting seagull, Carter's looks epitomise the cosmopolitan single male. Smart, tall, groomed, quick. This is a man with a mission statement, this is a man to whom stereotypes make the world a sensible place, this is a man with a big grin on his face and a Versace wallet in his pocket. Carter has been single for too long. Sure, he's had women, he thought to himself; but he wanted a young wife. *He yawns, sparkling blue eyes panning across the locals walking behind him.* Always live your life as if you are being watched. This was Carter-vision. The one man television network.

Brighton was big and powerful and smelt of contradiction, it was full of the business men and the low-lifes *He tries this voice-over again, a little deeper.* It wasn't as dirty as London and was brushed up against beautiful seaside. It reminded Carter of New York, but without the vast pretence. Hell, if there was something Carter couldn't stand about humans it was pretentiousness. *He winks at a petite lady walking a dog.* Today was the start of the weekend that Carter had decided was going to change his life. He was going to cook his mother a feast, take her to the opera and then dancing until dawn. Over cocktails on the beach, he was going to announce his intentions to find himself a young trophy bride by the Summer. Siree, this was the real ticket. Nearing St. James' Street, Carter stops along one of the narrow side roads. He quickly toys with the idea of stopping for a slim-line G & T in a small bar. He smiles with his decision; he would treat himself on the way home, providing that he gets all of the shopping done in half an hour. *He catches his reflection in the scratched perspex of a bus timetable. 'Charming', he revels in it for a moment .* Always a firm believer that everyone has a novel in them, Carter is planning his autobiography. He would be the first to admit that an autobiography is not strictly a novel, but would retort to any probes with his well-rehearsed answer: 'My life is as good as any fiction'. Oh boy, yes. Here is a man who is going to write the first warts-and-all autobiography of the average American go-getter. Entering through the supermarket doors, Carter suddenly doesn't feel impressive enough. He wants to tell everyone that he is a pioneer. He is the anti-celebrity. His dream is big. A large child bumps into Carter from behind, causing him to stumble into a rack of videos. The camera operator nearly stumble too, but balances himself on one leg – they'll have to cut that whole bit out (shame). *Carter Laine checks his reflection in the steel elevator door before making his way down towards the delicatessen.*

5.56 pm. Supermarket interior. Credit cards ping and pop.

In a few days it will be Halloween in Brighton & Hove, East Sussex, UK, Europe, The World, The Universe yada yada. The cosmopolitan seaside city will not be celebrating it this year. The three cameras are circling like flies on shit; the duty manager is looking edgy and confrontational as he watches them. They look like flies on shit, he thinks.

Ruth will probably be encouraging her Grandchildren to go trick or treating on the 31st. She will want to ply them with sweets and treats, but will be frowned upon by … Bronwyn. Ruth comes from an age where children were children and life was life. What all this nanny-noo nonsense that was spouted out all the time meant she had no idea: don't take pictures of your kids in the bath, don't call people coons, don't eat salmon. Society seemed somewhere else right now. No doubt, Ruth will have to say something to her daughter about the forthcoming weekend. 'Bronwyn, they need a bit of fun. Let them stuff their greedy little mouths. What you going to do, Bronwyn? Give them an extra bit of tofu for a treat? Poor things ...' She would think about this another day. There was still some shopping to do here. She got out her list and a passing housewife smiled (at least she looked like a housewife in those ridiculous council-estate leggings). Lard, strawberries, lamb, flour, cake icing, clothes pegs, orange juice....pumpkin. Yuck, they look like heads.

Alex was working like a Trojan. Due to lost grip on a newly opened cardboard outer, packets of savoury rice shower past her head. Fuck this. Alex is 5' 2" tall, unnaturally blonde, grey-blue eyes and prone to freckles. She's not that hot, she doesn't have that... appeal. But she'll do, and she knows that she can get what she wants; if she wants it. A large woman in her thirties looks at Alex for about twenty seconds from the other end of the aisle. Their eyes meet and then part. Alex stops herself from shouting 'urrr dyke', the woman moves quickly away. Halloween is stupid, American garbage, thinks Alex, missing the irony Alex will probably get drunk on Halloween. She will try to find a party and try to buy some pot. Alex will probably smoke too much and go green, but for the time being she has to earn her living; she wants to rearrange the fourth aisle. With a sudden feeling of control, she re-merchandises the shelves. I don't care what the plan is, thoughts drive through her square head, I am going to order the shelves my way. What a lark.

Carter holds a bottle of £17 Californian 2000 Merlot in one hand and a bottle of £15.99 Australian 1997 Chardonnay in the other. Disguising his indecision to the other customers in the crowded wine section, he chuckles and places both into his basket. He isn't prepared for the sudden weight gain on his left arm and attempts to make his bodily imbalance look decadent. It is nearly six o'clock. If he doesn't shop speedily, then he won't have time for his little gin therapy on the way home. *Carter walks to the bread counter watching the silver buckle on his moccasins reflect the bright white ceiling lights.* 'Laine...' Carter has a quick flashback to his Games teacher from High School, '...you have too many pairs of shoes for a boy.' For some reason this has always haunted him. A very firm believer that the shoes you wear determine your class, Carter feels much more at home in the UK; here it's good to acknowledge class and you can never have enough shoes. Tomorrow evening's proposed menu runs through his head with great zeal. Asparagus with sundried-tomato bread and paté followed by lamb and dill pancakes garnished with rocket salad. All topped at the end by profiteroles and fresh double cream and a rousing sing-a-long to a

Nana Mouskouri record. His mother would absolutely adore it. He picks up two soft 'Italian' ciabatta and places them in his basket. He has picked up the wine, the lamb, the herbs and the paté. He has eggs, milk, profiteroles, salad and cream waiting in the enormous Brighton sea front penthouse fridge back home. He only needs flour, and that was two aisles away. 'Not enough hours in the day', he mutters cheerfully to the elderly man on his left. The old man's response is not picked up on the microphone.

> *5.59 pm. The second hand breaks down.*
> *6.00 pm. Time. Stops. Forever.*

A sweeping camera shot of the Supermarket floor takes in every single person in every single aisle, behind every single till, counter and door. The air is quieter than death. Dust is flattening the tops of boxes, tins, tubs and a hundred million bright white lights seem to shine from every angle, casting shadows tall and black. To a stranger this could be heaven or hell. This is a picture of city life amongst the panic, the calm and the dizziness. In aisle one there is a boy crying and a crowd shows distaste. In aisle two there is a thin lady adding to her basket, which is already piled perilously high with leg-wax; another thin lady looks on, wide-eyed. Behind checkout six there is a uniformed man thinking about the colour beige, and a customer is waving a chequebook in his face. In the door way there is a group of ragged wanderers discussing Keats. The duty manager has been informed about these dirty beggars and is on his way.

If the camera were to focus in on a single shelf in aisle four, there would be a framed story there all by itself (and it's only due to a communication error that only one camera is in place). A microcosm of three hands; one wrinkled, one covered in black smudges, one recently cleansed laying awkwardly on top of a battered bag of flour. The only bag of flour visible. Three of society's aliens in a single moment at a single time. In an absurd anachronistic fantasy, a wicked witch, the tragic heroine and the handsome prince charming have been confronted with a conflict. There is plenty of flour in other shops all over Brighton, even a few seconds difference and the outcome could have been altered. Ruth's cake of independence, Alex's anarchic new stacking plan and Carter's fine, oedipal pancakes. Only each individual is aware of their own seriousness and each individual's reason is better than anyone else's. Parallax. And so … this single second in time is almost impossible. The director of the film would edit this scene carefully, flicking the view to a silent street outside. The flickering crisp packet in the wind is a visual pathetic fallacy; a beautiful testament to all that is suspended and awesome. The clumsy three around the flour murmur and grunt under their breath. All wanting to leave this nano-situation. All wanting one bag of flour.

Forever ends. Time goes past, and suddenly the scenario means nothing. A flash and there is someone else at the flour. Our three heroes have long gone. The checkouts and counters shout back to life, with even more fervour, as if capitalism will die without panic. The third cameraman's microphone picks up on the clacks and the pings of spend spend spend. The whirling hysteria of Brighton teatime reflect off of every stark, bleached wall. The director envisages the credits rolling, the world sees an ending ridden with pathos. Gentle music plays. Heading into a little side-road bar is an American queen in denial; handsome, arrogant. Checkout number two we see a brash little madam who is desperately misunderstood, and continually seeking more time. At the Old Steine bus stop number five, an old lady waits with her shopping bags and basket of apples, the bus driver rolls his eyes as she struggles with the step. Meanwhile a Supermarket should be closing; but it never will. A pumpkin tumbles from a vegetable stall and nobody picks it up.

Niall Gildea

Vocation

Idealized autumn morning. Dappled sunlight, *etc.*
"Detestable meteorology," I say in a posh voice.
Determinedly horizontal. Need to be vertical, or necessitate the assumption/establishment of verticality. Fuck's that moving around downstairs? Dog. Forgot that's still alive. Ugh. No food. Hard enough keeping me without feeding that. It could/might not/should fend for itself. Remove its collar and send it on its way. Sharp enough teeth. No trouble bringing down a cat or a child. Too early to do that. Can't be action yet – too soon. Need false sense of something first. Last evening's noodles'll have to do for now. But what of the future? What of it? Fucking southerners: Birmingham is *not* in the north. That is a linguistic fact. What is? All terminology, in the end. THE END. But it's not – let's face it.

Determined to determine to be vertical. Set alarm for five minutes hence and throw it out of reach. 1, elephant, 2, elephant, 3, elephant, 4, elephant, 5, elephant, 6, elephant, 7, elephant, 8, elephant, 9, elephant, 10, elephant, 11, elephant, 12, elephant, 13, elephant, 14, elephant, 15, elephant, 16, elephant, 17, elephant, 18, elephant, 19, elephant, 20, elephant, 21, elephant, 22, elephant, 23, elephant, 24, elephant, 25, elephant, 26, elephant, 27, elephant, 28, elephant, 29, elephant, 30, elephant, 31, elephant, 32, elephant, 33, elephant, 34, elephant, 35, elephant, 36, elephant, 37, elephant, 38, elephant, 39, elephant, 40, elephant, 41, elephant, 42, elephant, 43, elephant, 44, elephant, 45, elephant, 46, elephant, 47, elephant, 48, elephant, 49, elephant, 50, elephant, 51, elephant, 52, elephant, 53, elephant, 54, elephant, 55, elephant, 56, elephant, 57, elephant, 58, elephant, 59, elephant, 60, elephant. Repeat five times equals how it happened. <u>Alarm</u>. It's out of reach. Shit. I find my feet, sort of. Do my best. Pour cold tea in my bed so I won't want to re-enter. But I still do, obviously. Run out of the room screaming myself encouragement. Lock bedroom door from outside, and tape fingers together so I can't unlock it. Now what? Breakfast, but can't use an oven or a spoon with paddles for hands. Completely inadequate. Bugger. Used up the last of my cold tea on the bed. Breakfast will have to wait until tomorrow. Ugh. Dog. Forgot that's still alive. Might as well stroke it – nothing better to do. Now fur stuck in my tape. My hands look like a werewolf's are supposed to look. Except werewolves can wiggle their fingers. I'm just a wereplatypus.

Front door. Push. Been here forever and I still push the door first. Pull. That's it: enter the world. Daylight aches. Music; product placement! No music, no sound, nothing. Too late to be pissed off by the rush hour? No music. Bugger. Car. Fight with door; I normally win this one. No music. Establish that, and get in. Feels weird sober. Ugh. Don't thank me just because I stopped for you at a crossing. I'm legally obliged to do that. Too many pensioners in my life already. Maybe she's one who spends Christmas alone. Foot on the pedal: she wouldn't be missed, really. Turn her house into a sweetshop: not enough of those today. Like that one from that autobiography. I should write an autobiography. I should write *something*. Better than what I'm doing now: waiting for an old bitch to cross the road so I can carry on to something else shit. Always carrying on to something else shit. Something else shit is empirically all there is.

My empire is all I have, and that's something else shit too. Couldn't fight a war, or even route march. Decaying, decayed. All love me though. Wouldn't if they knew what I thought of them. Directionless, the lot of them. As am I, but I know it. Raining now. Freckled windscreen, *etc.*

"Detestable meteorology," I say in a posh voice.

Not my real voice. Not 'I', obviously. Always use the posh voice. Never used my real one – don't know what it sounds like. She's crossed, I can start moving again. Never actually stopped: just moved forward very slowly. Escaped this time. She'll probably drop dead soon anyway. Heart-attack, or maybe just a cold. World's well-equipped to do away with the old and shit. Life's not all bad. Only two more crossings to brave until I arrive. Hold myself back twice more. All right if nobody is on them. But somebody always is. Some body. Can't see anybody on either. Slow down a little; maybe somebody will arrive. Some body. Nobody there. No body. Drive on. How weird was last weekend? I shouldn't have let that happen; I'm sorry. You men, all the fucking same. I have my reasons, I really do. Bollocks. I won't pretend they're good reasons; but they're better than most. Bollocks. No body. Drive on. Carry on. Carry on to something else shit. Nearly there now.

Arrival. Car park. Some cunt's nicked my space. Not see the sign? Utterly directionless, the lot of them. Somebody already called them Emmets, so I must be right. Park all the way over here. A longer walk now. At least I'm not in my fucking costume yet. Groupies. Why does everybody say "Good morning"? Every body. I can form my own opinion re: the quality of the morning.

"Commendable meteorology," I say in a posh voice.

Past the groupies, past the windows which are not and never will be efficient at letting in light, and into my entrance. I forget the technical term. Begins with 'V', probably. Virgin, in theory anyway. Costume. Hanging up or down. Looks like a person with the innards sucked out. Fatality: Flawless Victory. Pull the person with the innards sucked out over my head. Got its innards back. Heart's beating now. Hear them entering, milling around, saying the same meaningless things as always. Tape still on my hands. Still a wereplatypus. Rip tape off. Still a wereplatypus. Hit face on wall, feel nose re-align. Still a wereplatypus. Trickle of blood. Sniff. Tastes like coins. Ready now. One hour and I can return to my bed. Back to the beginning. Filling up now, squawks quietening expectantly. Crack knuckles. Bell soon. Starting bell. Like I'm a fucking greyhound. Still a wereplatypus. <u>Bell</u>. Know my lines. Could I not know them? Don't know. Door. Pull. Been here forever and I still pull the door first. Push. That's it: enter the world. No question of the shroud this time. They are all staring. I want not to live. One hour and I can return to my bed, be determinedly horizontal again. No horizon, just flickering light and stares. Coughs. Hopefully the winter will turn those into something more. Something else shit. I'm in position. They wait, I wait. Book presented. I look down, don't read. I look up. I begin.

"In the name of the Father, and of the Son, and of the Holy Spirit," I say in a posh voice.

One hour. Then I'll go home and let the dog go.

About the Authors

Paul Thomas Abbott, aged 19, a first-year English student at St Anne's College, Oxford - lives (out of term-time) in Hampshire, born in Dorset.

Ned Beauman lives in London and is in his third year at Trinity, Cambridge reading Philosophy. In 2005 he won the RSC/Other Prize for new writing with his play *Camera Obscura*. He has written a novel. Also he wants to write comics and is looking for an artist.

Jonathan Birch is a Part IA Natural Scientist at Clare College, Cambridge. He is editor of the satirical student magazine *Clareification* and performs occasional stand-up comedy. The urban landscape of Manchester provides the backdrop for much of his writing.

Daisy Black is in her final year of studying English at Selwyn College, Cambridge. As well as being a keen writer, she has also been involved heavily with the drama scene and hopes to pursue a career in the theatre. Two of her short plays, *Anna's Answer* and *Making Tracks* have been produced during her time at Cambridge, but *Interior* is her first published piece of poetry.

Robert Crowe studies Classics at Lady Margaret Hall, Oxford University. He edited Cherwell in 2004. He has no plans for the future.

Denise Dooley has worked as a zinemaker, slam poet, playwright, 826 Valencia tutor and board member of Iowa City's James Gang. She is currently at work on a weeklong performance art piece on juvenilia and childhood rituals. She holds a BA from the University of Iowa and is completing an MPhil in English: Criticism and Culture at Cambridge.

Matthew Drage is a first year philosophy undergraduate at Homerton College, Cambridge. He was born in London, but has lived in the Midlands for most of his life. He likes to draw.

Niall Gildea, was born on 10/05/1987, but remembers even as a foetus being reticent re: writing autobiographically. Sixteen/seventeen years later, Niall and his school's Headmaster had frequent arguments about the length of his hair. Niall's hair – not the Headmaster's. The Headmaster didn't have hair; perhaps this was the real issue. He is now at Oxford.

Richard Freeman grew up in Brighton, Poole, Essex and Cambridge, but studied at Royal Holloway, University of London and Merton College, Oxford specialising in contemporary literature, drama and cultural theory. He writes stories and essays, but tends to write more for the theatre. Richard co-founded the Gobo Theatre Company in 1999.

Ted Hodgkinson is reading English at St. Edmund Hall, Oxford. His story *Figs Figures and Figureheads* was published in 2005. I don't write protest songs but, to quote Swift, "This work has made me of late years impatient for Peace, which I believe would save the lives of many brave words, as well as men." The possibility of being read is, to me, too good to be true. Ted's first novel is in the pipeline.

Bianca Jackson is a doctoral candidate at Wadham College, Oxford writing on the sexually dissident subject in contemporary Indian Anglophone literature. She is also the founding editor *Transgressions*, a forthcoming inter-disciplinary Arts and Humanities journal.

Charlotte Kingston is in her first year at Clare College, Cambridge, reading English. She sings in the chapel choir and enjoys oil paints, life modelling and chamber music.

Caleb Klaces is an undergraduate in his final year studying English at Oxford. He was twice a Poetry Society Young Poet of the Year and was once Young Poet of the Ledbury Poetry Festival. He comes from Birmingham.

James Knight likes James Joyce a bit too much. Joyce and Radiohead. And the NFL. In fact, he likes an awful lot of things. He just uses cynicism to disguise the fact that he's very easily pleased. He's a 2nd Year English student at Christ's College, Cambridge.

Muireann Maguire was born in 1979 and grew up near Dingle in Ireland. She did her B.A. at Trinity College Dublin and is now in Cambridge, working on a PhD in the area of 20th-century Russian literature. Her first poetry collection, *The Nightingale Seed*, was published by Lapwing Press in 2001.

Heather Mcrobie is a finalist in History and Politics at Keble College, Oxford, where she has spent most her time making dresses, performing stand-up, and sleeping. Next year she's studying Islamic Studies at McGill in Montreal, where she hopes to loiter in jazz bars, speak terrible French and stalk Leonard Cohen.

Ciaran O'Conaill is from Cork city, Ireland, and is currently studying Part III Mathematics at Cambridge. He has previously written material and music for performance, the most memorable being *The Volitional Brain*, a jazz-pop operetta.

Joelle Pedersen of Upton, Massachusetts is a visiting student from Boston College studying English and Theology at Mansfield College, Oxford. Ms. Pedersen hopes to pursue a career in education law. She enjoys running, theatre, Flannery O'Connor, and watching British people dance.

Ross Perlin, originally of New York City, studies Greek and Chinese philosophy at Corpus Christi College, Cambridge. Next year he will pursue an MA in Endangered Language Preservation at SOAS. Other interests include travel writing for historians of the future, the Polisario movement, and micro-graffiti.

Alex Steer was born in 1982 and read English at Girton College, Cambridge, where he has just completed an MPhil. in Medieval & Renaissance Literature. He has now moved to Oxford, where he is an Assistant Editor on the Oxford English Dictionary.

Timothy Thornton is a first-year music student at Pembroke College, Cambridge. Until university he concentrated almost exclusively on music, achieving at national level as a pianist and composer, but began writing after joining the college poetry society. He lives in Somerset.

Tom Wells is studying English at St Hugh's College, Oxford. He likes writing poems.

Anna Wilson is in the second year of a Classics degree at King's College, Cambridge. She spends far too much of her time watching trashy sci-fi TV and writing fanfiction, but maintains that her addiction is 'under control'. She comes from London.

Portobello
B O O K S

encouraging voices,
supporting writers,
challenging readers

'Portobello's intelligent risk-taking is more than a blessing.'
Ali Smith

'I'm pretty much expecting everything Portobello does to end
up in my Must Read pile.'
Douglas Coupland

'The times call for courage and Portobello has arrived. Get
ready for fearless publishing.'
Naomi Klein

www.portobellobooks.com